Understanding the Science of Climate Change

Talking Points – Impacts to the Eastern Woodlands and Forests

Natural Resource Report NPS/NRSS/CCRP/NRR—2011/470

Amanda Schramm
National Park Service Pacific West Region
909 First Avenue
Seattle, WA 98104

Rachel Loehman
Rocky Mountain Research Station
Fire Sciences Laboratory
5775 West US Hwy 10
Missoula, MT 59808-9361

With special thanks to the US Forest Service's Rocky Mountain Research Station and contributions from (in alphabetical order): Pat Campbell, Wendy Cass, Jim Comiskey, John Karish, David Manski, Brian Mitchell, Stephanie Perles, Susan Sachs, John Schmit, and Leigh Welling. Layout and design: Sara Melena, Angie Richman, Caitlin Shenk, and Katherine Stehli.

November 2011

U.S. Department of the Interior
National Park Service
Natural Resource Stewardship and Science
Fort Collins, Colorado

The National Park Service, Natural Resource Stewardship and Science office in Fort Collins, Colorado publishes a range of reports that address natural resource topics of interest and applicability to a broad audience in the National Park Service and others in natural resource management, including scientists, conservation and environmental constituencies, and the public.

The Natural Resource Report Series is used to disseminate high-priority, current natural resource management information with managerial application. The series targets a general, diverse audience, and may contain NPS policy considerations or address sensitive issues of management applicability.

All manuscripts in the series receive the appropriate level of peer review to ensure that the information is scientifically credible, technically accurate, appropriately written for the intended audience, and designed and published in a professional manner. This report received informal peer review by subject-matter experts who were not directly involved in the collection, analysis, or reporting of the data.

Views, statements, findings, conclusions, recommendations, and data in this report do not necessarily reflect views and policies of the National Park Service, U.S. Department of the Interior. Mention of trade names or commercial products does not constitute endorsement or recommendation for use by the U.S. Government.

This report is available from the Climate Change Response Program website: (http://www.nps.gov/climatechange/easternwoodlands.cfm), the Natural Resource Publications Management website: (http://www.nature.nps.gov/publications/NRPM) and the IRMA Portal: (https://irma.nps.gov/App/Reference/Profile/2181215).

Please cite this publication as:

Schramm, A. and R. Loehman. 2011. Understanding the science of climate change: talking points - impacts to the Eastern Woodlands and Forests. Natural Resource Report NPS/NRSS/CCRP/NRR—2011/470. National Park Service, Fort Collins, Colorado.

NPS909/111736, November 2011

Contents

I. Introduction

Purpose

Climate change presents significant risks to our nation's natural and cultural resources. Although climate change was once believed to be a future problem, there is now unequivocal scientific evidence that our planet's climate system is warming (IPCC 2007a). While many people understand that human emissions of greenhouse gases have significantly contributed to recent observed climate changes, fewer are aware of the specific impacts these changes will bring. This document is part of a series of bioregional summaries that provide key scientific findings about climate change and impacts to protected areas. The information is intended to provide a basic understanding of the science of climate change, known and expected impacts to resources and visitor experience, and actions that can be taken to mitigate and adapt to change. The statements may be used to communicate with managers, frame interpretive programs, and answer general questions from the public and the media. They also provide helpful information to consider in developing sustainability strategies and long-term management plans.

Audience

The Talking Points documents are primarily intended to provide park and refuge area managers and staff with accessible, up-to-date information about climate change and climate change impacts to the resources they protect.

Organizational Structure

Following the Introduction are three major sections of the document: a Regional Section that provides known and expected changes to the Eastern Woodlands and Forests, a section outlining No Regrets Actions that can be taken now to mitigate and adapt to climate changes, and a general section on Global Climate Change. The Regional Section is organized around seven types of changes or impacts, while the Global Section is arranged around four topics.

Regional Section

- Temperature
- The Water Cycle (including precipitation, snow, ice, and lake levels)
- Vegetation (plant cover, species range shifts, and phenology)
- Wildlife (aquatic and terrestrial animals, range shifts, invasive species, migration, and phenology)
- Disturbance (including range shifts, plant cover, plant pests and pathogens, fire, flooding, and erosion)
- Cultural Resources
- Visitor Experience

Global Section

- Temperature and Greenhouse Gases
- Water, Snow, and Ice
- Vegetation and Wildlife
- Disturbance

Information contained in this document is derived from the published results of a range of scientific research including historical data, empirical (observed) evidence, and model projections (which may use observed or theoretical relationships). While all of the statements are informed by science, not all statements carry the same level of confidence or scientific certainty. Identifying uncertainty is an important part of science but can be a major source of confusion for decision makers and the public. In the strictest sense, all scientific results carry some level of uncertainty because the scientific method can only "prove" a hypothesis to be false. However, in a practical world, society routinely elects to make choices and select options for actions that carry an array of uncertain outcomes.

The statements in this document have been organized to help managers and their staffs differentiate among current levels of uncertainty in climate change science. In doing so, the document aims to be consistent with the language and approach taken in the Fourth Assessment on Climate Change reports by the Intergovernmental Panel on Climate Change. However, this document discriminates among only three different levels of uncertainty and does not attempt to ascribe a specific probability to any particular level. These are qualitative rather than quantitative categories, ranked from greatest to least certainty, and are based on the following:

- "What scientists know" are statements based on measurable data and historical records. These are statements for which scientists generally have high confidence and agreement because they are based on actual measurements and observations. Events under this category have already happened or are very likely to happen in the future.

- "What scientists think is likely" represents statements beyond simple facts; these are derived from some level of reasoning or critical thinking. They result from projected trends, well tested climate or ecosystem models, or empirically observed relationships (statistical comparisons using existing data).

- "What scientists think is possible" are statements that use a higher degree of inference or deduction than the previous categories. These are based on research about processes that are less well understood, often involving dynamic interactions among climate and complex ecosystems. However, in some cases, these statements represent potential future conditions of greatest concern, because they may carry the greatest risk to protected area resources.

II. Climate Change Impacts to the Eastern Woodlands and Forests

The Eastern Woodlands and Forests bioregion that is discussed in this section is shown in the map to the right. A list of parks and refuges for which this analysis is most useful is included on the next page. To help the reader navigate this section, each category is designated by color-coded tabs on the outside edge of the document.

Federal Lands
- NPS
- FWS

Bioregions
- Arid Lands
- Atlantic Coast
- Boreal and Arctic
- Eastern Forests
- Great Lakes
- Gulf Coast
- Pacific Islands
- Maritime and Transitional
- Pacific Coast
- Prairie Grasslands and Potholes
- Western Mountains

Summary

The Eastern Woodlands and Forests bioregion is an expansive area with a diversity of forest types and associated ecosystems. Changes that have already been observed within this bioregion include warmer average annual temperatures, earlier dates of runoff, a longer frost-free period, and a longer growing season. During the 21st Century, warmer temperatures and increased water stress may affect forest health by reducing the amount and distribution of suitable habitat; . at the same time, these conditions may create suitable conditions for invasion of pests, pathogens, and exotic plant species. Climate changes may also affect wildlife species, including range shifts in mammals, birds, fish, and insects. Winter recreational activities may be altered by warmer winters with reduced snowfall, while autumn visitors will likely find that the fall foliage colors become less intense.

List of Parks and Refuges

U.S. National Park Service Units
- Abraham Lincoln Birthplace NHS
- Acadia NP
- Adams NHP
- Allegheny Portage Railroad NHS
- Andersonville NHS
- Andrew Johnson NHS
- Anacostia Park
- Antietam NB
- Appalachian NST
- Appomattox Court House NHP
- Arkansas Post NM
- Arlington House, The Robert E. Lee Memorial NHP
- Augusta Canal NHA
- Baltimore-Washington Parkway
- Big South Fork NRA
- Big Thicket NP
- Blackstone River Valley NHC
- Blue Ridge Parkway
- Bluestone NSR
- Booker T Washington NM
- Boston African American NHS
- Boston Harbor Islands NRA
- Boston NHP
- Brices Cross Roads NB
- Buffalo NR
- Cane River Creole NHP
- Cape Henry Memorial NHT
- Capitol Hill Parks
- Captain John Smith Chesapeake NHT
- Carl Sandburg Home NHS
- Carter G. Woodson Home NHS
- Catoctin Mountain Park
- Cedar Creek & Belle Grove NHP
- Central High School NHS
- Chattahoochee River NRA
- Chesapeake & Ohio Canal NHP
- Chesapeake Bay Gateways Network
- Chickamauga & Chattanooga NMP
- Civil War Defenses of Washington
- Claude Moore Colonial Farm
- Congaree NP
- Cowpens NB
- Cumberland Gap NHP

- Cuyahoga Valley NP
- David Berger NM
- Dayton Aviation Heritage NHP
- Delaware & Lehigh NHC
- Delaware NSR
- Delaware Water Gap NRA
- Deshler-Morris House
- Edgar Allan Poe NHS
- Effigy Mounds NM
- Eisenhower NHS
- Essex NHA
- First Ladies NHS
- Flight 93 NM
- Fort Donelson NB
- Fort Dupont Park
- Fort Foote Park
- Fort Necessity NB
- Fort Smith NHS
- Fort Washington Park
- Fredrick Douglass NHS
- Frederick Law Olmsted NHS
- Fredericksburg & Spotsylvania NMP
- Friendship Hill NHS
- Gauley River NRA
- George Rogers Clark NHP
- George Washington Birthplace NM
- George Washington Carver NM
- George Washington MP
- Gettysburg NMP
- Gloria Dei Church NHS
- Great Falls Park
- Great Smoky Mountains NP
- Greenbelt Park
- Green Springs NHLD
- Guilford Courthouse NMP
- Gullah/Geechee CHC
- Harmony Hall
- Harpers Ferry NHP
- Hopewell Culture NHP
- Hopewell Furnace NHS
- Horseshoe Bend NMP
- Hot Springs NP
- Independence NHP
- James A Garfield NHS
- Jamestown NHS

- Jefferson National Expansion Memorial
- Jimmy Carter NHS
- John F Kennedy NHS
- Johnstown Flood NM
- Kenilworth Park & Aquatic Gardens
- Kennesaw Mountain NB
- Kings Mountain NMP
- Lackawanna HV
- Langston Golf Course
- Lincoln Boyhood NM
- Little River Canyon NP
- Longfellow NHS
- Lowell NHP
- Lyndon Baines Johnson Memorial Grove on the Potomac
- Maggie L Walker NHS
- Maine Acadian Culture
- Mammoth Cave NP
- Manassas NB
- Marsh - Billings - Rockefeller NHP
- Martin Luther King Jr NHS
- Mary McLeod Bethune Council House NHS
- Minute Man NHP
- Monocacy NB

Acr	Unit Type
CHC	Cultural Heritage Corridor
FP	Forest Park
HA	Heritage Area
HV	Heritage Valley
MP	Memorial Parkway
NB	National Battlefield
NHA	National Heritage Area
NHC	National Heritage Corridor
NHLD	National Historic Landmark District
NHP	National Historic Park
NHS	National Historic Site
NHT	National Historic Trail
NHTR	National Heritage Tour Route
NM	National Monument
NMP	National Military Park
NP	National Park
NR	National River
NRA	National Recreation Area
NSR	National Scenic River
NST	National Scenic Trail
WSR	Wild & Scenic River
NWFR	National Wildlife and Fish Refuge
NWR	National Wildlife Refuge

List of Parks and Refuges Continued

- Moores Creek NB
- Morristown NHP
- Natchez NHP
- Natchez Trace NST
- Natchez Trace Parkway
- National Aviation HA
- New River Gorge NR
- Ninety Six NHS
- North Country NST
- Obed WSR
- Ocmulgee NM
- Oil Region NHA
- Overmountain Victory NHT
- Oxon Cove Park/Oxon Hill Farm
- Ozark NSR
- Path of Progress NHTR
- Pea Ridge NMP
- Perry's Victory & International Peace Memorial
- Petersburg NB
- Piscataway Park
- Potomac Heritage NST
- Poverty Point NM
- Prince William FP
- Quinebaug & Shetucket Rivers Valley NHC
- Richmond NB
- Rivers Of Steel NHA
- Rock Creek Park
- Roger Williams NM
- Roosevelt Campobello International Park
- Russell Cave NM
- Saint Croix Island International Historic Site
- Saint-Gaudens NHS
- Salem Maritime NHS
- Saratoga NHP
- Saugus Iron Works NHS
- Schuylkill River Valley NHA
- Selma To Montgomery NHT
- Sewall Belmont House and Museum
- Shenandoah NP
- Shiloh NMP
- Springfield Armory NHS
- Star-Spangled Banner NHT

- Steamtown NHS
- Stones River NB
- Tennessee Civil War NHA
- Thaddeus Kosciuszko NM
- Theodore Roosevelt Island Park
- Thomas Edison NHP
- Thomas Stone NHS
- Touro Synagogue NHS
- Trail Of Tears NHT
- Tupelo NB
- Tuskegee Airmen NHS
- Tuskegee Institute NHS
- Ulysses S. Grant NHS
- Upper Delaware Scenic and Recreational River
- Valley Forge NHP
- Vicksburg NMP
- Weir Farm NHS
- Wheeling NHA
- William Howard Taft NHS
- Wilson's Creek NB
- Wolf Trap National Park for the Performing Arts
- Yorktown NB

U.S. Fish & Wildlife Service Units
- Aroostook NWR
- Assabet River NWR
- Atchafalaya NWR
- Bald Knob NWR
- Banks Lake NWR
- Bayou Cocodrie NWR
- Big Lake NWR
- Big Oaks NWR
- Black Bayou Lake NWR
- Bogue Chitto NWR
- Bond Swamp NWR
- Cache River NWR
- Cahaba River NWR
- Canaan Valley NWR
- Carlton Pond Waterfowl Production Area
- Carolina Sandhills NWR
- Cat Island NWR
- Catahoula NWR

- Cherry Valley NWR
- Chickasaw NWR
- Choctaw NWR
- Clarence Cannon NWR
- Clarks River NWR
- Coldwater River NWR
- Crab Orchard NWR
- Cross Creeks NWR
- Cross Island NWR
- Cypress Creek NWR
- Dahomey NWR
- D'Arbonne NWR
- Driftless Area NWR
- Elizabeth Hartwell Mason Neck NWR
- Emiquon NWR
- Erie NWR
- Eufaula NWR
- Featherstone NWR
- Felsenthal NWR
- Fern Cave NWR
- Franklin Island NWR
- Grand Cote NWR
- Great Bay NWR
- Great Meadows NWR
- Great Swamp NWR
- Handy Brake NWR

Acr	Unit Type
CHC	Cultural Heritage Corridor
FP	Forest Park
HA	Heritage Area
HV	Heritage Valley
MP	Memorial Parkway
NB	National Battlefield
NHA	National Heritage Area
NHC	National Heritage Corridor
NHLD	National Historic Landmark District
NHP	National Historic Park
NHS	National Historic Site
NHT	National Historic Trail
NHTR	National Heritage Tour Route
NM	National Monument
NMP	National Military Park
NP	National Park
NR	National River
NRA	National Recreation Area
NSR	National Scenic River
NST	National Scenic Trail
WSR	Wild & Scenic River
NWFR	National Wildlife and Fish Refuge
NWR	National Wildlife Refuge

List of Parks and Refuges Continued

Temperature

- Hatchie NWR
- Hillside NWR
- Holla Bend NWR
- Holt Collier NWR
- James River NWR
- John H. Chafee NWR
- John Hay NWR
- John Heinz NWR at Tinicum
- Key Cave NWR
- Lake Isom NWR
- Lake Ophelia NWR
- Little River NWR
- Logan Cave NWR
- Lower Hatchie NWR
- Mashpee NWR
- Massasoit NWR
- Mathews Brake NWR
- Meredosia NWR
- Middle Mississippi NWR
- Mingo NWR
- Mississippi Sandhill Crane NWR
- Moosehorn NWR
- Morgan Brake NWR
- Mountain Longleaf NWR
- Muscatatuck NWR
- Nansemond NWR
- Neches River NWR
- Ninigret NWR
- Noxubee NWR
- Occoquan Bay NWR
- Ohio River Islands NWR
- Overflow NWR
- Oxbow NWR
- Ozark Cavefish NWR
- Ozark Plateau NWR
- Panther Swamp NWR
- Parker River NWR
- Patoka River NWR and Management Area
- Patuxent NWR
- Pee Dee NWR
- Petit Manan NWR
- Piedmont NWR
- Pilot Knob NWR
- Pocosin Lakes NWR
- Pond Creek NWR

- Pond Island NWR
- Presquile NWR
- Rachel Carson NWR
- Rappahannock River Valley NWR
- Red River NWR
- Reelfoot NWR
- Roanoke River NWR
- Sachuest Point NWR
- Santee NWR
- Sauta Cave NWR
- Seal Island NWR
- Sequoyah NWR
- Shawangunk Grasslands NWR
- Silvio O. Conte NFWR
- St. Catherine Creek NWR
- Stewart B. McKinney NWR
- Sunkhaze Meadows NWR
- Susquehanna River NWR
- Tallahatchie NWR
- Tennessee NWR
- Tensas River NWR
- Thacher Island NWR
- Theodore Roosevelt NWR
- Trempealeau NWR
- Trinity River NWR
- Trustom Pond NWR
- Two Rivers NWR
- Umbagog NWR
- Upper Ouachita NWR
- Upper Mississippi River NFWR
- Waccamaw NWR
- Wallkill NWR
- Wapack NWR
- Wapanocca NWR
- Watercress Darter NWR
- Wheeler NWR
- White River NWR
- Yazoo NWR

Acr	Unit Type
CHC	Cultural Heritage Corridor
FP	Forest Park
HA	Heritage Area
HV	Heritage Valley
MP	Memorial Parkway
NB	National Battlefield
NHA	National Heritage Area
NHC	National Heritage Corridor
NHLD	National Historic Landmark District
NHP	National Historic Park
NHS	National Historic Site
NHT	National Historic Trail
NHTR	National Heritage Tour Route
NM	National Monument
NMP	National Military Park
NP	National Park
NR	National River
NRA	National Recreation Area
NSR	National Scenic River
NST	National Scenic Trail
WSR	Wild & Scenic River
NWFR	National Wildlife and Fish Refuge
NWR	National Wildlife Refuge

A. Temperature

What scientists know....

- Temperature and precipitation extremes become more pronounced in the Northeast region (northeastern United States) between 1926 and 2000, with most of this increase occurring over the past four decades (Griffiths and Bradley 2007).

- Average temperatures in the midwestern United States have also shown a notable increase in recent decades (USGCRP 2009).

- The frost-free season in the Midwest has become longer in recent decades, and has increased by as much as two weeks since the beginning of the century (Wuebbles and Hayhoe 2004).

- Winters are warming more rapidly than summers in both the Northeast and Midwest regions. Winter mean, minimum, and maximum air temperatures in the northeast region increased at a rate between 0.42 °C (0.77° F) and 0.46 ° C (0.83° F) per decade between 1965 and 2005, with the greatest warming occurring in January and February, typically the coldest months of winter (Burakowski et al. 2008; Hayhoe et al. 2006; USGCRP 2009).

- The Northeast experienced an increase in extremely warm days (the number of days that exceed the 95th percentile threshold for daily maximum temperature) and a decrease in extremely cold temperature days over the course of the 20th Century (1900-1996)(DeGaetano and Allen 2002).

What scientists think is likely...

- Temperatures are predicted to increase in the Northeast and Midwest in the future. In the Northeast region, annual regional surface temperatures are projected to increase by 2.9 °C (5.2 °F) to 5.3 °C (9.5 °F) by 2070-2099 relative to the 1961-1999 time period. By the end of the century, annual average daily maximum temperatures in the Midwest may increase between 2 °C and 9 °C (3.6 °F to 16 °F). These projections are based on different scenarios of greenhouse gas emissions, with lower changes in temperature associated with lower emissions (Hayhoe et al. 2007; Wuebbles and Hayhoe 2004).

- Regional climate projections for the Northeastern and Southeastern United States for the late 21st century include increased frequency of extreme heat events, decreased frequency of extreme cold events, and decreased severity of cold events (Diffenbaugh et al. 2005).

- The frost-free season in the Midwest is expected to continue to lengthen, possibly by as much as 4 to 8 weeks over the course of the 21st Century (Wuebbles and Hayhoe 2004).

What scientists think is possible...

- By 2090, the Midwestern United States may experience 20 to 50 more days per year of temperatures over 32 °C (58 °F) compared to current conditions, and 40 to 75 fewer days per year below freezing (Wuebbles and Hayhoe 2004).

- Models indicate that summer temperatures may increase as much or more than winter temperatures. This may be due to regional-scale feedbacks in the water balance such as a decrease in snow-albedo (decreased reflection of radiation/heat as snow cover is reduced) and increased warming due to increased evaporation (Hayhoe et al. 2007; Wuebbles and Hayhoe 2004).

We acknowledge the NOAA GFDL CM2.1, NCAR/DOE PCM and UKMet HadCM3 modeling groups for making available the atmosphere-ocean general circulation model data.

We also acknowledge Ed Maurer and Katharine Hayhoe for the statistical downscaling; ATMOS Research & Consulting for data analysis and graphics; and the Union of Concerned Scientists for support of this work.

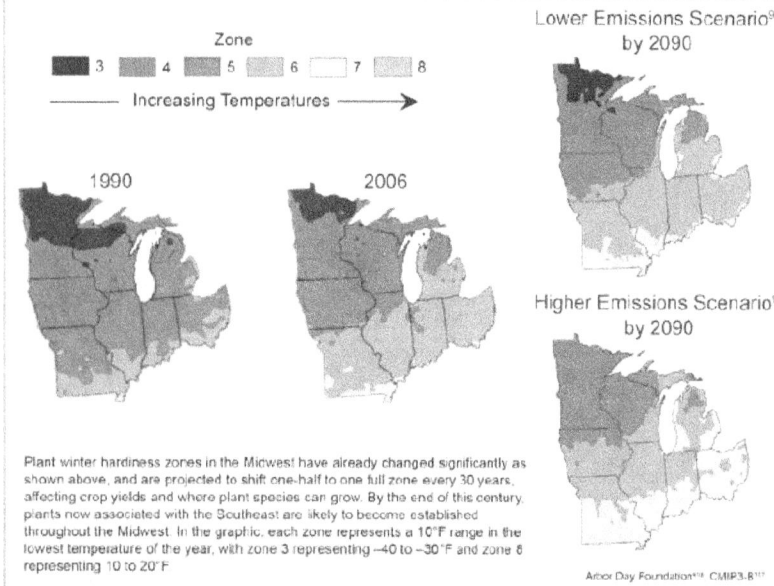

Plant winter hardiness zones in the Midwest have already changed significantly as shown above, and are projected to shift one-half to one full zone every 30 years, affecting crop yields and where plant species can grow. By the end of this century, plants now associated with the Southeast are likely to become established throughout the Midwest. In the graphic, each zone represents a 10°F range in the lowest temperature of the year, with zone 3 representing -40 to -30°F and zone 8 representing 10 to 20°F

Arbor Day Foundation[a] CMIP3-R[b]

View looking "upstream" of Big Run at U.S. 340 on southwest side of Shenandoah National Park following an extended period of drought; USGS photo.

Temperature

Water Cycle

Vegetation

Wildlife

Disturbance

Cultural Resources

Visitor Experience

B. THE WATER CYCLE

What scientists know....

- The Northeast has experienced increases in both average annual rainfall and heavy precipitation (rainfall of more than 2 inches in 48 hours) since the 1980s (Hayhoe et al. 2007). Heavy precipitation events have also increased in the Midwest over the past century (Wuebbles and Hayhoe 2004).

- Annual average snowfall decreased in the Northeast in the last half of the 20th Century and into the early 21st Century, as has the ratio of snow to total precipitation. Records from Historical Climatology Network sites indicate both an average decrease in the amount of snow over most of New England from 1949 to 2000, as well as an average decrease in the ratio of snow to total precipitation recorded in much of the region; in other words, an increased amount of winter precipitation in the form of rain versus snow (Huntington et al. 2004). Snow level records from Maine show that decreases in snowpack depth from 1954 to 2004 at most locations (Hodgkins and Dudley 2006).

- An earlier onset of hydrologic indicators of spring has occurred in the Northeast region, including earlier onset of lake ice-out, river ice-out, and snowmelt-driven spring runoff (Huntington et al. 2003).

What scientists think is likely....

- Stream flow extremes are expected to increase, including a general tendency toward higher winter and spring streamflows and reduced summer and fall stream flows. The tendency toward increased winter high-flow events, and reduced summer low-flow events is likely to become more pronounced. Different warming scenarios result in different degrees to which stream flow will likely change in the future (Hayhoe et al. 2007; Huntington et al. 2003).

- Winter-season runoff is projected to increase with warmer and wetter winters, spring runoff is expected to decrease, and an overall increase is projected in annual runoff rates as peak runoff shifts to earlier in the year (Hayhoe et al. 2007).

What scientists think is possible....

- By the end of the 21st century, average winter precipitation in the northeastern United States is projected to increase between 20% and 30%, but summer precipitation may decrease only slightly as compared with current levels (Hayhoe et al. 2008). Over the same time period, the frequency of heavy precipitation events in the Midwest may as much as double (Wuebbles and Hayhoe 2004).

- Increasing temperatures may promote more rapid summer plant development, potentially placing additional stresses on water resources in the Northeast. Increased temperatures and longer growing seasons could increase evapotranspiration (evaporation combined with plant transpiration) and reduce runoff, altering the timing of the hydrological cycle and impacting water quality (USDA 2001; Hayhoe et al. 2007).

- Warmer temperatures are expected to cause an increase in evaporation. The bulk of increased evaporation is projected to occur during the spring and summer, and could significantly impact the vulnerability of the region to drought in combination with factors such as changes in precipitation, runoff, and soil moisture (Hayhoe et al. 2007).

Due to the growing season lasting longer and the number of frost days decreasing, flowering and dormancy seasons are shifting for many plant species. (Top): Fall colors in Shenandoah NP; (Bottom): Mountain Laural in Great Smoky Mountains NP; NPS Photos.

C. VEGETATION

What scientists know....

- The growing season has been lengthening and spring is arriving earlier in the year, as compared to historical data. The average length of winter freeze has been decreasing, and frost days have declining in the US. With first freeze occurring later and last freeze occurring earlier over the course of the 20th century, the result has been a longer growing season (Hayhoe et al. 2007).

- Several spring events, including bud burst and flowering, have been occurring earlier in the year on the North American continent (Hayhoe et al. 2007; Parmesan, 2006a).

- Studies of a northeast forest system have shown that changes in plant species abun-

dance is strongly correlated with flowering-time response. Species that do not respond to temperature shifts, including asters and campanulas (Asterales), bluets (Rubiaceae p.p.), bladderworts (Lentibulariaceae), dogwoods (Cornaceae), lilies (Liliales), mints (Lamiaceae p.p.), roses (Rosaceae p.p.) have declined in abundance (Willis et al. 2008).

- Climate has demonstrably affected terrestrial ecosystems through changes in the seasonal timing of life-cycle events (phenology), plant growth responses (primary production), and biogeographic distribution (Field et al. 2007; Parmesan 2006b). Statistically significant shifts in Northern Hemisphere vegetation phenology, productivity, and distribution have been observed and are attributed to 20th century climate changes (Parmesan 2006b; Parmesan and Yohe 2003; Walther et al. 2002).

- Tree-ring data from five oak species in the southeastern Appalachian forest, aged at between 135 and 300 years, indicate that summer growing season drought is the most important factor for limiting oak growth (Speer et al. 2009). Population declines and increased mortality among oaks, especially those related to red oaks, have been observed from Missouri to South Carolina, corresponding to multi-year and seasonal droughts in the 1980s through the 2000s (Allen et al. 2010).

- Prolonged winter thaws followed by sharp freezing are an important factor in causing shoot dieback of northern hardwood species. Analysis of such thaw-freeze events between 1930 and 2000 showed that the pattern of thaw-freeze events corresponded to dieback and decline of yellow birch (Bourque et al. 2005). Prolonged warm seasons followed by abrupt cold snaps can similarly harm vegetation, as mild winters or warm, early springs cause plants to prematurely develop, exposing vulnerable plant tissues to the freezing conditions. The northeast experienced an event like this in 2007, with resulting damage to natural vegetation as well as agricultural crops (Gu et al. 2008).

- A study chronicling 150 years of plant data in Massachusetts shows that invasive

Temperature

Water Cycle

Vegetation

Wildlife

Disturbance

Cultural Resources

Visitor Experience

Temperature

Water Cycle

Vegetation

Wildlife

Disturbance

Cultural Resources

Visitor Experience

Tree species that thrive in cooler conditions, such as this Virginia Round-leaf birch are projected to lose habitat in the Northeast and shift largely into Canada; NPS photo.

plants have been far more effective than native plants at adjusting flowering times to changing climatic conditions (Hayhoe et al. 2007; Iverson and Prasad 2002; Willis et al. 2010).

What scientists think is likely....

- Climate change models predict higher maximum temperatures and more extreme precipitation events, and because plants rely on specific ranges of temperature and precipitation, longer drought periods, increased flooding events, and heat waves outside of the normal range may cause stress. In addition, less predictable winter temperature and precipitation patterns with periods of warming may cause trees and other vegetation to come out of dormancy and begin early growth, which increases their vulnerability to future seasonal cold temperatures (Winnett 1998; USDA 2001).

- DNA evidence suggests that tree migrations since the last glaciation were much slower than the rate that is needed to keep up with the current and projected future rates of climate warming (Mohan et al. 2009).

- Observed correlations among heat, drought, and tree mortality are consistent with the probability that climate change is contributing to increased tree mortality. Rising temperatures and increasingly severe drought conditions can combine to increase forest stress and contribute to accelerated mortality (Allen et al. 2010).

- Warmer temperatures could affect flowering, fruit set, and/or seed production of many plant species. A longer growing season could result in increased wood production and decreased roots and foliar mass for northeastern North American forest trees. While an earlier spring and longer growing season can increase plant production, too much heat and a shortened, warmer winter can decrease production and hinder reproduction. If temperatures exceed the threshold for certain species for even short periods, critical flowering and pollination periods can be affected. (Campbell et al. 2009; Hayhoe et al. 2007; Wolfe et al. 2008).

What scientists think is possible....

- Modeling of 134 tree species in the eastern United States showed that by the end of the 21st century, suitable habitat may expand by at least 10% for approximately 66 tree species, and decrease by at least 10% for 54 species, with most of the habitat moving generally northeast. Vulnerability to habitat loss and gain increase as CO_2 emissions levels rise (Iverson et al. 2008).

- Tree species that thrive in cooler conditions, such as sugar maple (Acer saccharum) and birch (Betula), are projected to lose habitat in the Northeast, shifting largely to Canada. Oaks (Quercus), hickories (Carya), and pines (Pinus) may experience an expansion of potential habitat. However, expansion may be limited by soil properties and seed dispersal. Modeling also suggests a retreat of the spruce-fir

(Picea-Abies) zone and advancement of southern oaks and pines by the end of the century (Parmesan 2006a; USDA 2001; Iverson et al. 2008). Suitable habitat for Spruce/Fir forest may all but disappear from the northeastern United States under a high-emissions scenario, and spruce/fir forest productivity is expected to decline even under a low emissions scenario. The small but sensitive alpine tundra areas of the Northeast are similarly threatened (Frumhoff et al. 2007).

• Forests in the Northeast may become more productive, while the Southeast might experience dieback. A longer growing season along with increased temperatures and increases in CO_2 could increase forest growth. At the same time, species distributions may change, with trees and other vegetation that are more suited to warmer weather moving eastward and northward. If other competing disturbances, such as forest fire, insects and disease are not overwhelming, then smaller increases in temperature, increased CO_2, and longer growing seasons could promote forest growth in the Northeast (USDA 2001).

• Chronic forest stress and mortality risk may increase in coming decades due to warmer temperatures, more frequent heat waves, and more frequent or longer-term regional drought conditions (Allen et al. 2010).

• Warmer temperatures may exacerbate the effects of ozone pollution on forest growth, including reduced growth, reduced seed production and increased vulnerability to disease (USDA 2001).

• Modeling shows that large increases in temperature and decreases in precipitation in the eastern United States could result in an average of about 11% of total ecosystem carbon being released into the atmosphere by the end of the century. Fire suppression would likely reduce this carbon loss, but would not create a carbon sink (a situation where the ecosystem absorbs carbon) without both a high CO_2 level and a high growth sensitivity to CO_2 (Lenihan et al. 2008).

• Modeling of climate change effects on Tennessee forests for 2030 and 2080 shows changes in tree diversity and species composition in all of the state's ecological provinces, with the greatest changes in the Southern Mixed Forest province (Dale et al. 2010).

D. WILDLIFE

What scientists know....

• A meta-analysis of climate change effects on range boundaries in Northern Hemisphere species of birds, butterflies, and alpine herbs shows an average shift of 6.1 kilometers (3.8 miles) per decade northward, and a mean shift toward earlier onset of spring events (frog breeding, bird nesting, first flowering, tree budburst, and arrival of migrant butterflies and birds) of 2.3 days per decade (Parmesan and Yohe 2003).

• Studies of migratory bird patterns in New York for 1980 to 1985 and 2000 to 2005 showed that all 129 species of birds studied have shifted their range northward over time (Zuckerberg et al. 2009).

• Since 1961, migratory birds at a banding station in western Pennsylvania have shown a steady decrease in body size, including decreased fat-free mass and wing chord, consistent with a response to a warmer climate (Van Buskirk et al. 2010).

• Based on 33 years of bird capture data between 1970 and 2002, migratory bird groups have shrunk in size; these groups

Migratory birds at a banding station in western Pennsylvania have shown a steady decrease in body size, including decreased fat-free mass and wing chord, consistent with a response to a warmer climate. A juvenile Peregrine Falcon is banded at Acadia NP in Maine; NPS photo.

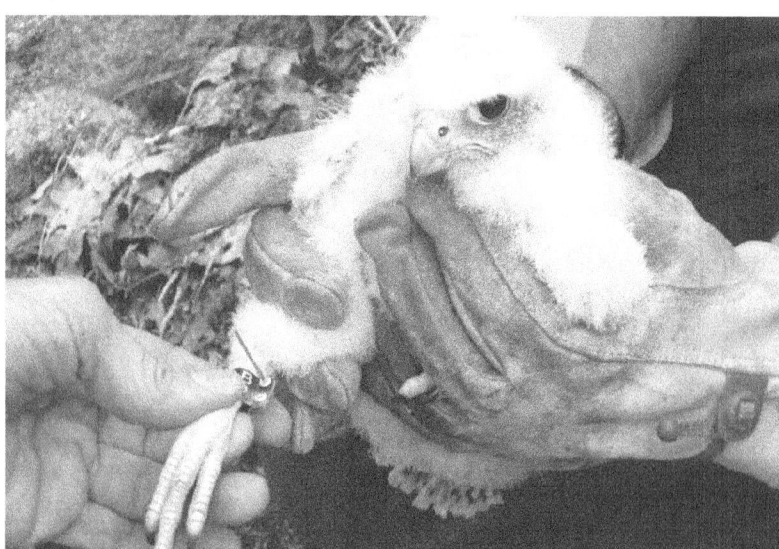

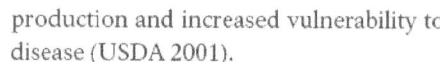

Temperature

Water Cycle

Vegetation

Wildlife

Disturbance

Cultural Resources

Visitor Experience

have trended toward earlier spring arrival dates (Miller-Rushing et al. 2008).

What scientists think is likely....

- The disruption of coordination in timing between lifecycles of predators and prey may be the greatest impact on wildlife due to climate change (Parmesan 2006a).

- Eastern forest bird species show proportionately higher vulnerability to climate change than birds in western, boreal, or subtropical forests. About 75% of eastern forest bird species that are restricted to a single forest type show medium or high vulnerability to observed and projected impacts of climate change (NABCI 2010).

- A study of five tree species of the eastern United States (persimmon [Diospyros virginiana], sweetgum [Liquidambar styraciflua], sourwood [Oxydendrum arboretum], loblolly pine [Pinus taeda], and southern red oak [Quercus falcate varfalcata]) shows that future species migrations

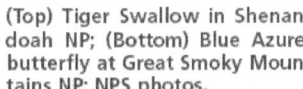

(Top) Tiger Swallow in Shenandoah NP; (Bottom) Blue Azure butterfly at Great Smoky Mountains NP; NPS photos.

in the eastern United States will likely differ from the past due to habitat loss and fragmentation, reducing the natural system's ability to respond to global change. In the past, species have migrated through intact forests. Human development has divided forest lands and fragmented habitats. This will make migration of species trying to adapt to changing temperature and precipitation more difficult (Iverson et al. 2004).

- Based on observed and projected species range shifts due to climate change, the richness of both mammal and bird populations is expected to generally decrease in the southern United States and increase in cooler mountainous areas. In general, species richness may decline in the short term even in areas where it is expected to increase in the long term, as some species disappear from the area and others migrate toward it (Currie 2001).

- Insect species in high-latitude locations have a relatively broad heat tolerance and generally live in climates that are currently cooler than is optimal, so warming temperatures are unlikely to harm, and may even enhance, their fitness. The same may be true for some cold-blooded vertebrate species (Deutsch et al. 2008).

What scientists think is possible....

- Due to vegetation shifts and thus habitat shifts, parks may experience a shift in mammalian species at a greater rate than anything documented in the geological record. Researchers have concluded that rapid changes are possible, and could potentially occur over periods of 20 to 50 years. Under a doubling of atmospheric CO_2, projections showed potential for species turnover at Acadia National Park (approximately 6.9% species loss, with overall turnover of 5 species), Shenandoah National Park (approximately 9.0% species loss, with overall turnover of 8 species), and most notably Great Smoky Mountains National Park (approximately 16.7% species loss, with overall turnover of 21 species) (Burns et al. 2003).

- An analysis of potential climate change impacts on mammalian species in U.S.

Drought conditions in the Eastern Mountains have increased the forest fire hazards; NPS photo.

national parks indicates that on average about 8% of current mammalian species diversity may be lost. The greatest losses across all parks would occur in rodent species (44%), bats (22%), and carnivores (19%) (Burns et al. 2003).

- In general, forest birds may fare better than other bird species in adapting to climate change due to their large range and high reproductive potential, with the exception of those that depend on highly seasonal resources, high elevation, extremely humid, or riparian forests (NABCI, 2010).

- Birds that migrate only a short distance (e.g., those that winter in the southern United States from northern regions) may be quicker to adapt to climate change than long-distance migrants that spend their winters south of the United States, since short-distance migrants can identify and respond to meteorological cues indicating northern weather conditions, while long-distance migrants must rely on photoperiod to indicate when they should migrate (Butler 2003; Miller-Rushing et al.,2008).

- As birds shift their ranges to higher elevation to compensate for changing climatic conditions, their risk of extinction may increase. Models indicate that with a warming of 2.8 °C (5 °F), as many as

550 Western Hemisphere land bird species may lose enough suitable habitat to become extinct, and approximately 2,150 additional species would be at risk of extinction by the year 2100 (Sekercioglu et al. 2007).

- Potential impacts to trout populations due to climate change is complex, and influenced by a variety of factors that could result in both increases and decreases in populations. Models suggest that rising temperatures alone may result in increased abundance of brook and rainbow trout, while a combination of increases in water temperature and flow could result in population decreases in some areas. Factoring in events such as floods could cause a net loss of rainbow trout (Clark et al. 2001). When availability of suitable habitat is factored into modeling, results show that increasing temperatures could result in a significant loss of habitat area, which could result in increased fragmentation of trout populations,rendering them vulnerable to extirpation (Flebbe et al. 2006).

E. DISTURBANCE

What scientists know....

- During the 1980s and the period between 1998 and 2002, drought conditions in the Southern Appalachian Mountains led to a rise in average area burned (Lafon et al. 2005).

- Black-legged tick (Ixodes scapularis) is a carrier of Borrelia burgdorferi, the bacteria that causes Lyme disease. The seasonality of black-legged tick host seeking is directly correlated to climate, and specifically to warm temperatures (Gatewood et al. 2009). In fact, many nuisance species benefit from warmer temperatures. When water limitation is not a factor, temperature increases can increase metabolism, reproductive rates, and survival of nuisance species (Dukes et al. 2009).

- Outbreaks of southern pine beetle extended into northern forests during the period from 1960 to 2004 at the same time that extreme minimum temperatures in the

Temperature

Water Cycle

Vegetation

Wildlife

Disturbance

Cultural Resources

Visitor Experience

southeastern United States experienced a warming trend, increasing minimum winter air temperatures by 3.3 °C (Tran et al. 2007).

What scientists think is likely....

- Projections identify drier and hotter summers and more frequent short or medium-term droughts. Cumulatively, these could significantly impact the water supply and stress vegetation including agriculture and forests (Hayhoe et al. 2007).

- Rising temperatures are likely to increase forest fire hazards, increase the length of the fire season, and contribute to larger fires. This could in turn increase atmospheric carbon contributions from forests (USDA 2001).

- Climate has a strong seasonal and interannual influence on the fire regime of the Central Appalachians including effects on number of fires, area burned, and fire intensity. As a result, changes in climate are expected to alter the existing fire regime (Lafon et al. 2005).

- Warming temperatures can increase problems related to insects and disease. For

The seasonality of nuisance species like the black-legged tick may benefit from warmer temperatures; Photo copyright Steve Jacobs, Pennsylvania State University.

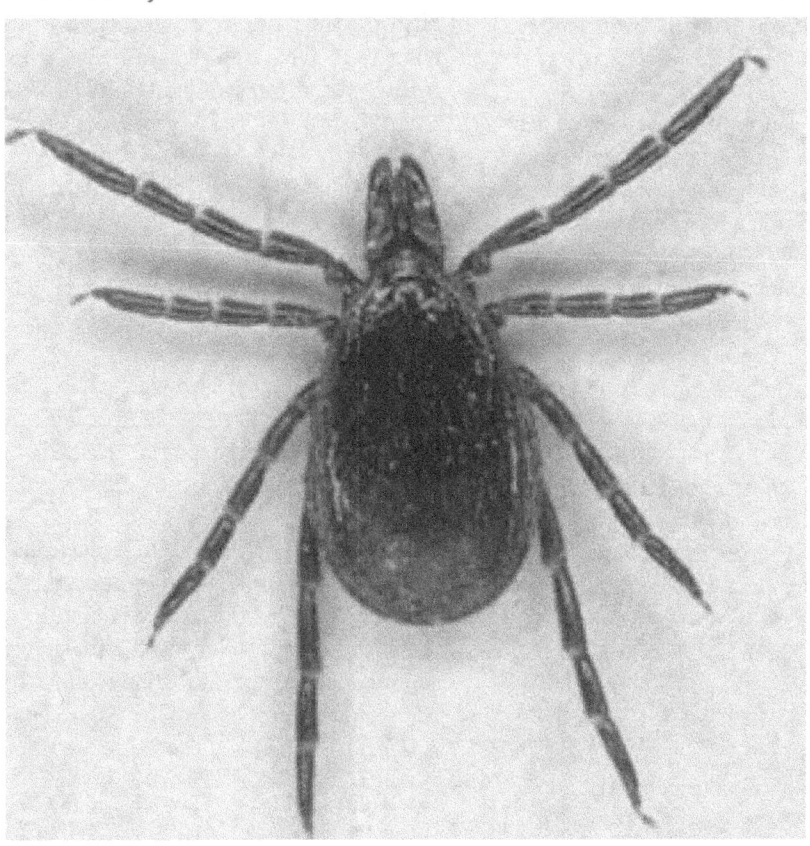

example, changes in climate are likely to affect the seasonality of black-legged tick and, as a result, the spread of Lyme disease. In addition, because insects and pathogens have shorter life spans than most forest vegetation, they can respond more rapidly to climate change. A longer growing season may mean that more generations of pests are present to attack vegetation, while a shorter and warmer winter may mean more successful over-wintering for pests and relatively larger populations in spring. Vegetation that has been stressed by drought or fire is also more susceptible to disease and infestation, increasing vulnerability to attack (USDA 2001; Hayhoe et al. 2007; Winnett 1998; Gatewood et al. 2009).

- Climate change is likely to increase the growth and reproduction of some forest pathogens, as well as affecting their dispersal, transmission, infection phenology, and overwinter survival. For example, increases in extreme temperatures are likely to further increase the range of the southern pine beetle in northeastern North America (Dukes et al. 2009).

What scientists think is possible....

- Predicted increases in drought frequency, duration, and severity, as well as heat stress associated with climate changes, could fundamentally alter the composition, structure, and biogeography of forests (Allen et al. 2010).

- Loss of coastal wetlands due to sea level rise increases the vulnerability of inland ecosystems to storm disturbance. Increasingly intense windstorms may penetrate farther into forested areas than has historically been the case. Taken together, rising sea levels and increasing intensity and frequency of windstorm events could affect the ecosystem services (e.g., carbon sequestration, nutrient retention, erosion control) of coastal and inland forests and alter their relationship with intertidal wetlands (Hopkinson et al. 2008).

- Nitrogen and sulfate deposition alters forest nutrient availability and retention, reduces reproductive success and frost

Historic structures, like the red canons at Saratoga NHP, are vulnerable to changes in temperature, wind, and moisture; Photo courtesy of Jacquie Tinkler.

hardiness, causes leaf damage, and affects forest pest and disease patterns. As the climate warms, these processes in combination may increase tree declines and ecosystem disturbances in the northeastern United States (Mohan et al. 2009).

- With climate warming, infestation of hemlock wooly adelgid (Adelges tsugae), a pest that is already linked to declines in hemlock (Tsuga)populations, may spread unimpeded throughout the range of North American hemlock. Armillaria mellea, or honey fungus, a common fungus that has been associated with sugar maple mortality, could spread throughout every forest type in North America (Dukes et al. 2009).

- In some cases, climate change may actually reduce pestilence in some areas, such as the warmer edges of current habitat areas or areas where pests overwinter in forest litter and rely on snow depth for survival (Dukes et al. 2009).

F. CULTURAL RESOURCES

What scientists know....

- Historic structures are vulnerable to changes in temperature, wind, and moisture as well as infestation of pests (UNESCO 2007).

- Preservation of archeological resources in the earth depends on a delicate balance of conditions. Changes to these conditions may reduce the chance of artifacts' survival (UNESCO 2007).

- Benefits of using local knowledge and traditional practices in resource management can help facilitate adaptation to climate change (Finucane 2009; IPCC 2008).

- Land use areas that are fixed in place, like national parks and Native American reservations, are particularly vulnerable to the effects of climate change because they cannot adapt by relocating in response to changes in natural conditions (Smith et al. 2001).

Temperature

Water Cycle

Vegetation

Wildlife

Disturbance

Cultural Resources

Visitor Experience

Temperature

Water Cycle

Vegetation

Wildlife

Disturbance

Cultural Resources

Visitor Experience

G. VISITOR EXPERIENCE

What scientists know....

- A recent survey found that more people in the Northeast participate in outdoor recreation during winter when the weather is cold and snowy (Frumhoff et al. 2007).

What scientists think is likely....

- The locations of climatically ideal tourism conditions are likely to shift toward higher latitudes under projected climate change, and as a consequence redistribution in the locations and seasons of tourism activities may occur. The effects of these changes will depend greatly on the flexibility demonstrated by institutions and tourists as they react to climate change (Amelung et al. 2007).

(Top) A ranger conducting a wildflower program, (Bottom) A hiker enjoying the view at Shenandoah NP; NPS photos.

- Reduction in snowpack could significantly reduce opportunities for winter recreational activities that are popular in the northeastern United States, such as skiing and snowmobiling (Frumhoff et al. 2007; Scott et al. 2008).

- An increase in frequency of drought conditions in forests of the northeastern United States will likely result in decreased intensity of fall foliage coloration (Huntington et al. 2009).

- Changes in runoff, stream flow, and trout distribution will likely affect fishing opportunities (Frumhoff et al. 2007).

What scientists think is possible....

- By the end of the century, reliable ski seasons may become limited to northern New York and parts of Vermont, New Hampshire, and western Maine. A higher emissions scenario shows even further geographic restrictions, with suitable ski areas located only in the northern New England states and northern New York by mid-century. Under this scenario, only western Maine would have a reliable ski season by the end of the century (Frumhoff et al. 2007).

- Increased atmospheric CO_2 in combination with warmer temperatures and changes in precipitation in the northeastern United States may alter the growth patterns of both plant-based and fungal allergens, with implications for allergy and asthma sufferers both indoors and outdoors (Ziska et al. 2008).

- Parks and refuges may not be able to meet their mandate of protecting current species within their boundaries, or in the case of some refuges, the species for whose habitat protection they were designed. While wildlife may be able to move northward or to higher elevations to escape some effects of climate change, federal land boundaries are static (Burns et al. 2003).

III. No Regrets Actions: How Individuals, Parks, Refuges, and Their Partners Can Do Their Part

Individuals, businesses, and agencies release carbon dioxide (CO_2), the principal greenhouse gas, through burning of fossil fuels for electricity, heating, transportation, food production, and other day-to-day activities. Increasing levels of atmospheric CO_2 have measurably increased global average temperatures, and are projected to cause further changes in global climate, with severe implications for vegetation, wildlife, oceans, water resources, and human populations. Emissions reduction – limiting production of CO_2 and other greenhouse gases - is an important step in addressing climate change. It is the responsibility of agencies and individuals to find ways to reduce greenhouse gas emissions and to educate about the causes and consequences of climate change, and ways in which we can reduce our impacts on natural resources. There are many simple actions that each of us can take to reduce our daily carbon emissions, some of which will even save money.

Agencies Can...

Improve sustainability and energy efficiency

- Use energy efficient products, such as ENERGY STAR® approved office equipment and light bulbs.

- Initiate an energy efficiency program to monitor energy use in buildings. Provide guidelines for reducing energy consumption. Conserve water.

- Convert to renewable energy sources such as solar or wind generated power.

- Specify "green" designs for construction of new or remodeled buildings.

- Include discussions of climate change in the park Environmental Management System.

- Conduct an emissions inventory and set goals for CO_2 reduction.

- Provide alternative transportation options such as employee bicycles and shuttles for within-unit commuting.

- Provide hybrid electric or propane-fueled vehicles for official use, and impose fuel standards for park vehicles. Reduce the number and/or size of park vehicles and boats to maximize efficiency.

- Provide a shuttle service or another form of alternate transportation for visitor and employee travel to and within the unit.

- Provide incentives for use of alternative transportation methods.

- Use teleconferences and webinars or other forms of modern technology in place of travel to conferences and meetings.

Implement Management Actions

- Engage and enlist collaborator support (e.g., tribes, nearby agencies, private landholders) in climate change discussions, responses, adaptation and mitigation.

- Develop strategies and identify priorities for managing uncertainty surrounding climate change effects in parks and refuges.

- Dedicate funds not only to sustainable actions but also to understanding the impacts to the natural and cultural resources.

- Build a strong partnership-based foundation for future conservation efforts.

- Identify strategic priorities for climate change efforts when working with partners.

- Incorporate anticipated climate change impacts, such as decreases in lake levels or changes in vegetation and wildlife, into management plans.

An interpretive brochure about climate change impacts to National Parks was created in 2006 and was distributed widely. This brochure was updated in 2008.

Climate Change in National Parks

Park Service employees install solar panels at San Francisco Maritime National Historical Park (Top); At the National Mall, Park Service employees use clean-energy transportation to lead tours; NPS photos.

- Encourage climate change research and scientific study in park units and refuges.

- Design long-term monitoring projects and management activities that do not rely solely on fossil fuel-based transportation and infrastructure.

- Incorporate products and services that address climate change in the development of all interpretive and management plans.

- Take inventory of the facilities/boundaries/species within your park or refuge that may benefit from climate change mitigation or adaptation activities.

- Participate in gateway community sustainability efforts.

- Recognize the value of ecosystem services that an area can provide, and manage the area to sustain these services. Conservation is more cost-effective than restoration and helps maintain ecosystem integrity.

- Provide recycling options for solid waste and trash generated within the park.

Restore damaged landscapes

- Strategically focus restoration efforts, both in terms of the types of restoration undertaken and their national, regional, and local scale and focus, to help maximize resilience.

- Restore and conserve connectivity within habitats, protect and enhance instream flows for fish, and maintain and develop access corridors to climate change refugia.

- Restoration efforts are important as a means for enhancing species' ability to cope with stresses and adapt to climatic and environmental changes. Through restoration of natural areas, we can lessen climate change impacts on species and their habitats. These efforts will help preserve biodiversity, natural resources, and recreational opportunities.

- Address climate change impacts to cultural resources by taking actions to document, preserve, and recover them.

Educate staff and the public

- Post climate change information in easily accessible locations such as on bulletin boards and websites.

- Provide training for park and refuge employees and partners on effects of climate change on resources, and on dissemination of climate change knowledge to the public.

- Support the development of region, park, or refuge-specific interpretive products on the impacts of climate change.

- Incorporate climate change research and information in interpretive and education outreach programming.

- Distribute up-to-date interpretive products (e.g., the National Park Service-wide Climate Change in National Parks brochure).

- Develop climate change presentations for local civic organizations, user and partner conferences, national meetings, etc.

- Incorporate climate change questions and answers into Junior Ranger programs.

- Help visitors make the connection between reducing greenhouse gas emissions and resource stewardship.

- Encourage visitors to use public or non-motorized transportation to and around parks.

> "Humankind has not woven the web of life. We are but one thread within it. Whatever we do to the web, we do to ourselves. All things are bound together. All things connect."
> —Chief Seattle

- Encourage visitors to reduce their carbon footprint in their daily lives and as part of their tourism experience.

Individuals can...

- In the park or refuge park their car and walk or bike. Use shuttles where available. Recycle and use refillable water bottles. Stay on marked trails to help further ecosystem restoration efforts.

- At home, walk, carpool, bike or use public transportation if possible. A full bus equates to 40 fewer cars on the road. When driving, use a fuel-efficient vehicle.

- Do not let cars or boats idle - letting a car idle for just 20 seconds burns more gasoline than turning it off and on again.

- Replace incandescent bulbs in five most frequently used light fixtures in the home with bulbs that have the ENERGY STAR® rating. If every household in the U.S. takes this one action we will prevent greenhouse gas emissions equivalent to the emissions from nearly 10 million cars, in addition to saving money on energy costs.

Reduce, Reuse, Recycle, Refuse

- Use products made from recycled paper, plastics and aluminum - these use 55-95% less energy than products made from scratch.

- Purchase a travel coffee mug and a reusable water bottle to reduce use of disposable products (Starbucks uses more than 1 billion paper cups a year).

- Carry reusable bags instead of using paper or plastic bags.

- Recycle drink containers, paper, newspapers, electronics, and other materials. Bring recyclables home for proper disposal when recycle bins are not available. Rather than taking old furniture and clothes to the dump, consider "recycling" them at a thrift store.

- Keep an energy efficient home. Purchase ENERGY STAR® appliances, properly insulate windows, doors and attics, and lower the thermostat in the winter and raise it in the summer (even 1-2 degrees makes a big difference). Switch to green power generated from renewable energy sources such as wind, solar, or geothermal.

- Buy local goods and services that minimize emissions associated with transportation.

- Encourage others to participate in the actions listed above.

- Conserve water.

For more information on how you can reduce carbon emissions and engage in climate-friendly activities, check out these websites:

EPA- What you can do: http://www.epa.gov/climatechange/wycd/index.html

NPS- Climate Change Response Program: http://www.nps.gov/climatechange

NPS- Do Your Part! Program: http://www.nps.gov/climatefriendlyparks/doyourpart.html

US Forest Service Climate Change Program: http://www.fs.fed.us/climatechange/

United States Global Change Research Program: http://www.globalchange.gov/

U.S. Fish and Wildlife Service Climate change: http://www.fws.gov/home/climatechange/

The Climate Friendly Parks Program is a joint partnership between the U.S. Environmental Protection Agency and the National Park Service. Climate Friendly Parks from around the country are leading the way in the effort to protect our parks' natural and cultural resources and ensure their preservation for future generations; NPS image.

IV. Global Climate Change

The IPCC is a scientific intergovernmental, international body established by the World Meteorological Organization (WMO) and by the United Nations Environment Programme (UNEP). The information the IPCC provides in its reports is based on scientific evidence and reflects existing consensus viewpoints within the scientific community. The comprehensiveness of the scientific content is achieved through contributions from experts in all regions of the world and all relevant disciplines including, where appropriately documented, industry literature and traditional practices, and a two stage review process by experts and governments.

Definition of climate change: The IPCC defines climate change as a change in the state of the climate that can be identified (e.g. using statistical tests) by changes in the mean and/or the variability of its properties, and that persists for an extended period, typically decades or longer. All statements in this section are synthesized from the IPCC report unless otherwise noted.

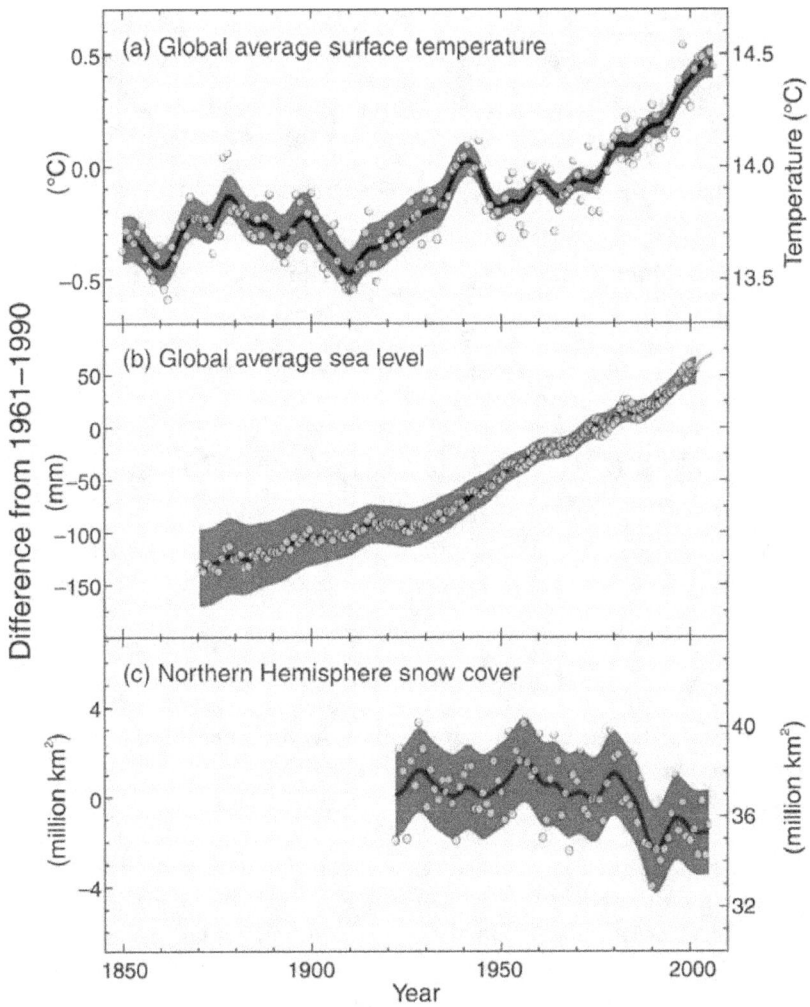

Figure 1. Observed changes in (a) global average surface temperature; (b) global average sea level from tide gauge (blue) and satellite (red) data and (c) Northern Hemisphere snow cover for March-April. All differences are relative to corresponding averages for the period 1961-1990. Smoothed curves represent decadal averaged values while circles show yearly values. The shaded areas are the uncertainty intervals estimated from a comprehensive analysis of known uncertainties (a and b) and from the time series (c) (IPCC 2007a).

A. Temperature and Greenhouse Gases

What scientists know...

• Warming of the Earth's climate system is unequivocal, as evidenced from increased air and ocean temperatures, widespread melting of snow and ice, and rising global average sea level (Figure 1).

• In the last 100 years, global average surface temperature has risen about 0.74°C over the previous 100-year period, and the rate of warming has doubled from the previous century. Eleven of the 12 warmest years in the instrumental record of global surface temperature since 1850 have occurred since 1995 (Figure 1).

• Although most regions over the globe have experienced warming, there are regional variations: land regions have warmed faster than oceans and high northern latitudes have warmed faster than the tropics. Average Arctic temperatures have increased at almost twice the global rate in the past 100 years, primarily because loss of snow and ice results in a positive feedback via increased absorption of sunlight by ocean waters (Figure 2).

• Over the past 50 years widespread changes in extreme temperatures have been observed, including a decrease in cold days and nights and an increase in the frequency of hot days, hot nights, and heat waves.

• Winter temperatures are increasing more rapidly than summer temperatures, particularly in the northern hemisphere, and

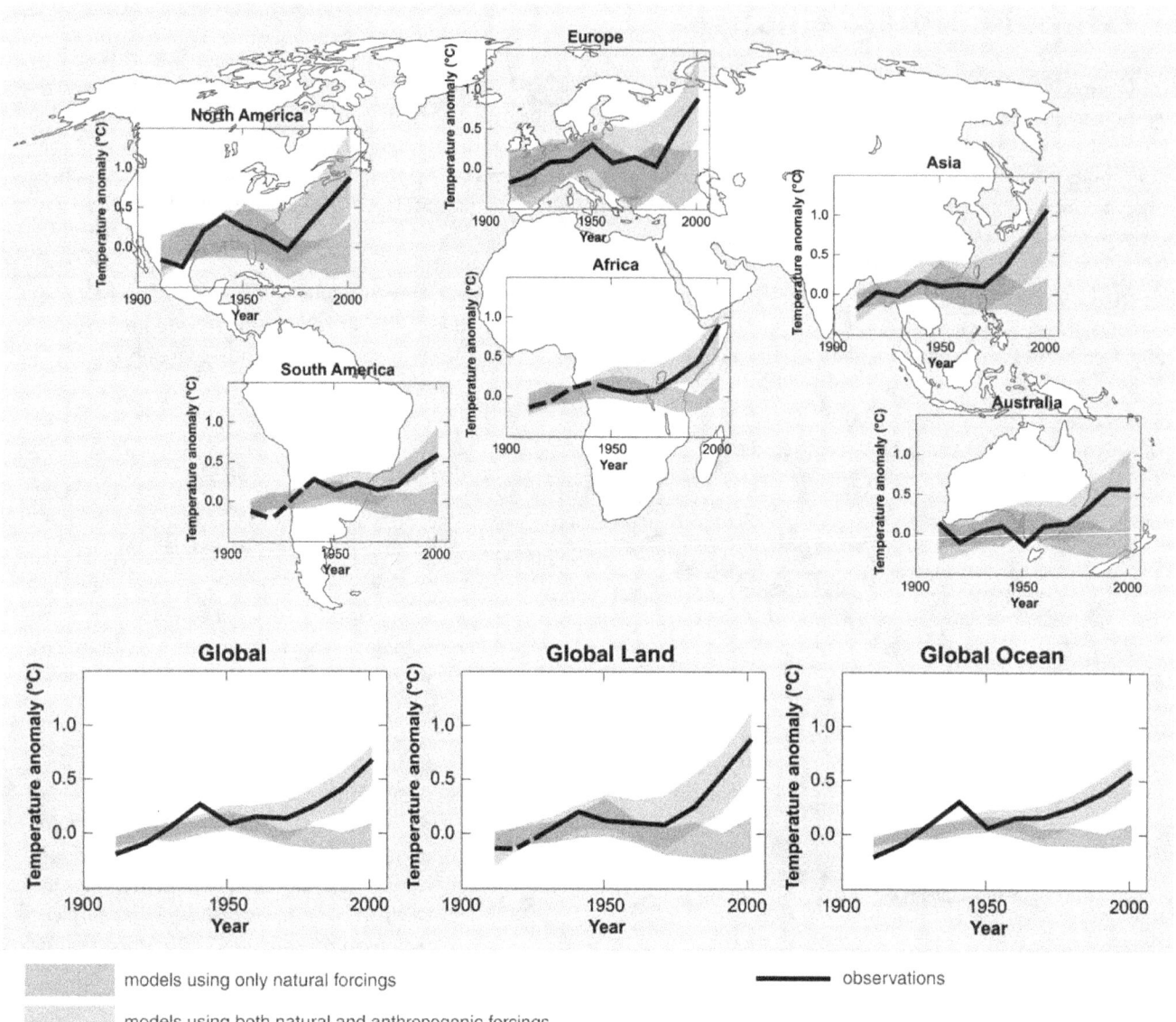

models using only natural forcings

models using both natural and anthropogenic forcings

━━━ observations

Figure 2. Comparison of observed continental- and global-scale changes in surface temperature with results simulated by climate models using either natural or both natural and anthropogenic forcings. Decadal averages of observations are shown for the period 1906-2005 (black line) plotted against the centre of the decade and relative to the corresponding average for the period 1901-1950. Lines are dashed where spatial coverage is less than 50%. Blue shaded bands show the 5 to 95% range for 19 simulations from five climate models using only the natural forcings due to solar activity and volcanoes. Red shaded bands show the 5 to 95% range for 58 simulations from 14 climate models using both natural and anthropogenic forcings (IPCC 2007a).

there has been an increase in the length of the frost-free period in mid- and high-latitude regions of both hemispheres.

- Climate change is caused by alterations in the energy balance within the atmosphere and at the Earth's surface. Factors that affect Earth's energy balance are the atmospheric concentrations of greenhouse gases and aerosols, land surface properties, and solar radiation.

- Global atmospheric concentrations of greenhouse gases have increased significantly since 1750 as the result of human activities. The principal greenhouse gases are carbon dioxide (CO_2), primarily from fossil fuel use and land-use change; methane (CH_4) and nitrous oxide (N_2O), primarily from agriculture; and halocarbons

(a group of gases containing fluorine, chlorine or bromine), principally engineered chemicals that do not occur naturally.

- Direct measurements of gases trapped in ice cores demonstrate that current CO_2 and CH_4 concentrations far exceed the natural range over the last 650,000 years and have increased markedly (35% and 148% respectively), since the beginning of the industrial era in 1750.

- Both past and future anthropogenic CO_2 emissions will continue to contribute to warming and sea level rise for more than a millennium, due to the time scales required for the removal of the gas from the atmosphere.

- Warming temperatures reduce oceanic uptake of atmospheric CO_2, increasing the fraction of anthropogenic emissions remaining in the atmosphere. This positive carbon cycle feedback results in increasingly greater accumulation of atmospheric CO_2 and subsequently greater warming trends than would otherwise be present in the absence of a feedback relationship.

- There is very high confidence that the global average net effect of human activities since 1750 has been one of warming.

- Scientific evidence shows that major and widespread climate changes have occurred with startling speed. For example, roughly half the north Atlantic warming during the last 20,000 years was achieved in only a decade, and it was accompanied by significant climatic changes across most of the globe (NRC 2008).

What scientists think is likely...

- Anthropogenic warming over the last three decades has likely had a discernible influence at the global scale on observed changes in many physical and biological systems.

- Average temperatures in the Northern Hemisphere during the second half of the 20th century were very likely higher than during any other 50-year period in the last 500 years and likely the highest in at least the past 1300 years.

- Most of the warming that has occurred since the mid-20th century is very likely due to increases in anthropogenic greenhouse gas concentrations. Furthermore, it is extremely likely that global changes observed in the past 50 years can only be explained with external (anthropogenic) forcings (influences) (Figure 2).

- There is much evidence and scientific consensus that greenhouse gas emissions will continue to grow under current climate change mitigation policies and development practices. For the next two decades a warming of about 0.2°C per decade is projected for a range of emissions scenarios; afterwards, temperature projections increasingly depend on specific emissions scenarios (Table 1).

- It is very likely that continued greenhouse gas emissions at or above the current rate will cause further warming and result in changes in the global climate system that will be larger than those observed during the 20th century.

- It is very likely that hot extremes, heat waves and heavy precipitation events will become more frequent. As with current trends, warming is expected to be greatest over land and at most high northern latitudes, and least over the Southern Ocean (near Antarctica) and the northern North Atlantic Ocean.

What scientists think is possible...

- Global temperatures are projected to increase in the future, and the magnitude of temperature change depends on specific emissions scenarios, and ranges from a 1.1°C to 6.4°C increase by 2100 (Table 1).

Table 1. Projected global average surface warming at the end of the 21st century, adapted from (IPCC 2007b).

Notes: a) Temperatures are assessed best estimates and likely uncertainty ranges from a hierarchy of models of varying complexity as well as observational constraints. b) Temperature changes are expressed as the difference from the period 1980-1999. To express the change relative to the period 1850-1899 add 0.5°C. c) Year 2000 constant composition is derived from Atmosphere-Ocean General Circulation Models (AOGCMs) only.

Emissions Scenario	Temperature Change (°C at 2090 – 2099 relative to 1980 – 1999)[a,b]	
	Best Estimate	Likely Range
Constant Year 2000 Concentrations[a]	0.6	0.3 – 0.9
B_1 Scenario	1.8	1.1 – 2.9
B_2 Scenario	2.4	1.4 – 3.8
A_1B Scenario	2.8	1.7 – 4.4
A_2 Scenario	3.4	2.0 – 5.4
A_1F_1 Scenario	4.0	2.4 – 6.4

Figure 3. Sea ice concentrations (the amount of ice in a given area) simulated by the GFDL CM2.1 global coupled climate model averaged over August, September and October (the months when Arctic sea ice concentrations generally are at a minimum). Three years (1885, 1985 & 2085) are shown to illustrate the model-simulated trend. A dramatic reduction of summertime sea ice is projected, with the rate of decrease being greatest during the 21st century portion. The colors range from dark blue (ice free) to white (100% sea ice covered); Image courtesy of NOAA GFDL.

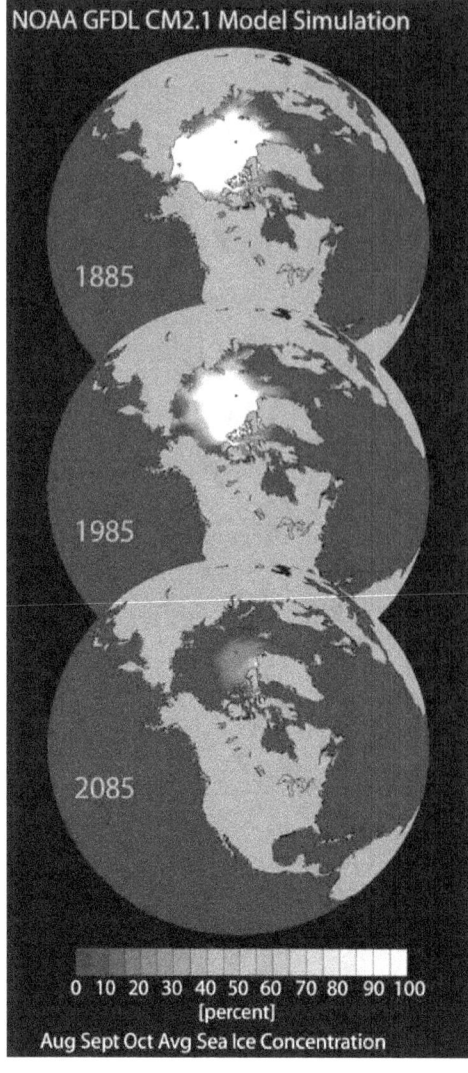

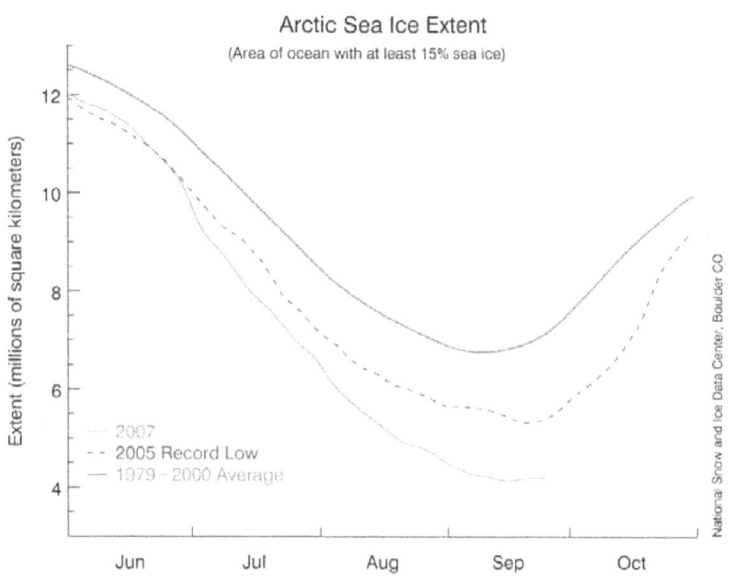

Figure 4. Arctic sea ice in September 2007 (blue line) is far below the previous low record year of 2005 (dashed line), and was 39% below where we would expect to be in an average year (solid gray line). Average September sea ice extent from 1979 to 2000 was 7.04 million square kilometers. The climatological minimum from 1979 to 2000 was 6.74 million square kilometers (NSIDC 2008).

• Anthropogenic warming could lead to changes in the global system that are abrupt and irreversible, depending on the rate and magnitude of climate change.

• Roughly 20-30% of species around the globe could become extinct if global average temperatures increase by 2 to 3°C over pre-industrial levels.

B. Water, Snow, and Ice

What scientists know...

• Many natural systems are already being affected by increased temperatures, particularly those related to snow, ice, and frozen ground. Examples are decreases in snow and ice extent, especially of mountain glaciers; enlargement and increased numbers of glacial lakes; decreased permafrost extent; increasing ground instability in permafrost regions and rock avalanches in mountain regions; and thinner sea ice and shorter freezing seasons of lake and river ice (Figure 3).

• Annual average Arctic sea ice extent has shrunk by 2.7% per decade since 1978, and the summer ice extent has decreased by 7.4% per decade. Sea ice extent during the 2007 melt season plummeted to the lowest levels since satellite measurements began in 1979, and at the end of the melt season September 2007 sea ice was 39% below the long-term (1979-2000) average (NSIDC 2008)(Figure 4).

• Global average sea level rose at an average rate of 1.8 mm per year from 1961 to 2003 and at an average rate of 3.1 mm per year from 1993 to 2003. Increases in sea level since 1993 are the result of the following contributions: thermal expansion, 57%; melting glaciers and ice caps, 28%, melting polar ice sheets, 15%.

• The CO_2 content of the oceans increased by 118 ± 19 Gt (1 Gt = 109 tons) between A.D. 1750 (the end of the pre-industrial period) and 1994 as the result of uptake of anthropogenic CO_2 emissions from the atmosphere, and continues to increase by about 2 Gt each year (Sabine et al. 2004; Hoegh-Guldberg et al. 2007). This increase in oceanic CO_2 has resulted in a 30% increase in acidity (a decrease in surface ocean pH by an average of 0.1 units), with observed and potential severe negative consequences for marine organisms and coral reef formations (Orr et al. 2005: McNeil and Matear 2007; Riebesell et al. 2009).

• Oceans are noisier due to ocean acidification reducing the ability of seawater to absorb low frequency sounds (noise from ship traffic and military activities). Low-frequency sound absorption has decreased over 10% in both the Pacific and Atlantic over the past 200 years. An assumed additional pH drop of 0.3 (due to anthropogenic CO_2 emissions) accompanied with warming will lead to sound absorption below 1 kHz being reduced by almost half of current values (Hester et. al. 2008).

• Even if greenhouse gas concentrations are stabilized at current levels thermal expansion of ocean waters (and resulting sea level rise) will continue for many centuries, due to the time required to transport heat into the deep ocean.

• Observations since 1961 show that the average global ocean temperature has increased to depths of at least 3000 meters, and that the ocean has been taking up over 80% of the heat added to the climate system.

• Hydrologic effects of climate change include increased runoff and earlier spring peak discharge in many glacier- and snow-fed rivers, and warming of lakes and rivers.

• Runoff is projected to increase by 10 to 40% by mid-century at higher latitudes and in some wet tropical areas, and to decrease by 10 to 30% over some dry regions at mid-latitudes and dry tropics. Areas in which runoff is projected to decline face a reduction in the value of the services provided by water resources.

• Precipitation increased significantly from 1900 to 2005 in eastern parts of North and South America, northern Europe, and northern and central Asia. Conversely, precipitation declined in the Sahel, the Mediterranean, southern Africa, and parts of southern Asia (Figure 5).

What scientists think is likely....

• Widespread mass losses from glaciers and reductions in snow cover are projected to accelerate throughout the 21st century, reducing water availability and changing seasonality of flow patterns.

• Model projections include contraction of snow cover area, widespread increases in depth to frost in permafrost areas, and Arctic and Antarctic sea ice shrinkage.

• The incidence of extreme high sea level has likely increased at a broad range of sites worldwide since 1975.

• Based on current model simulations it is very likely that the meridional overturning circulation (MOC) of the Atlantic Ocean will slow down during the 21st century; nevertheless regional temperatures are predicted to increase. Large-scale and persistent changes in the MOC may result in changes in marine ecosystem productivity,

Figure 5. Relative changes in precipitation (in percent) for the period 2090-2099, relative to 1980-1999. Values are multi-model averages based on the SRES A$_1$B scenario for December to February (left) and June to August (right). White areas are where less than 66% of the models agree in the sign of the change and stippled areas are where more than 90% of the models agree in the sign of the change (IPCC 2007a).

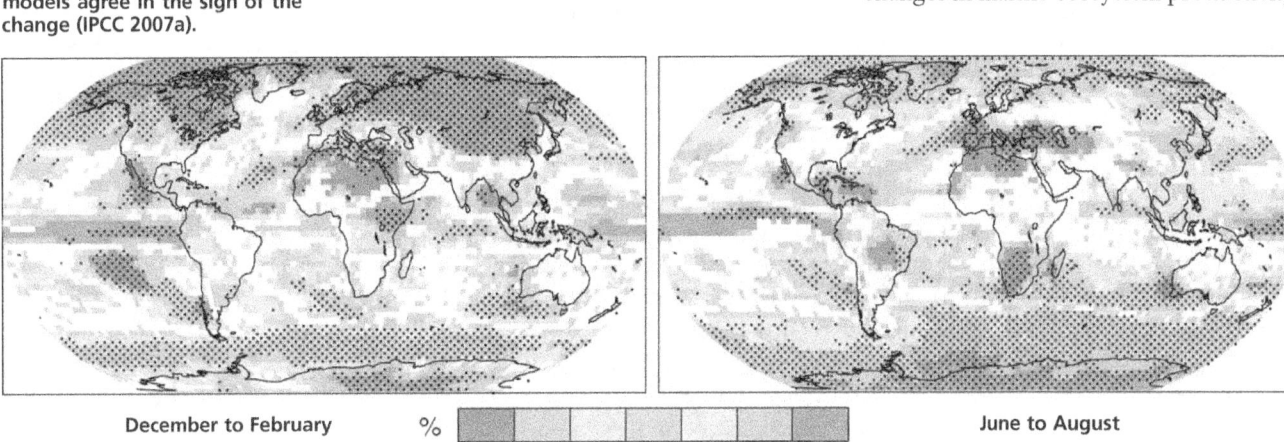

December to February   %   June to August

-20   -10   -5   5   10   20

Table 2. Projected global average sea level rise at the end of the 21st century, adapted from IPCC 2007b.

Notes: a) Temperatures are assessed best estimates and likely uncertainty ranges from a hierarchy of models of varying complexity as well as observational constraints.

Emissions Scenario	Sea level rise (m at 2090 – 2099 relative to 1980 – 1999)
	Model-based range (excluding future rapid dynamical changes in ice flow)
Constant Year 2000 Concentrations[a]	0.3 – 0.9
B_1 Scenario	1.1 – 2.9
B_2 Scenario	1.4 – 3.8
A_1B Scenario	1.7 – 4.4
A_2 Scenario	2.0 – 5.4
A_1F_1 Scenario	2.4 – 6.4

fisheries, ocean CO_2 uptake, and terrestrial vegetation.

- Globally the area affected by drought has likely increased since the 1970s and the frequency of extreme precipitation events has increased over most areas.

- Future tropical cyclones (typhoons and hurricanes) are likely to become more intense, with larger peak wind speeds and increased heavy precipitation. Extra-tropical storm tracks are projected to move poleward, with consequent shifts in wind, precipitation, and temperature patterns.

- Increases in the amount of precipitation are very likely in high latitudes and decreases are likely in most subtropical land regions, continuing observed patterns (Figure 5).

- Increases in the frequency of heavy precipitation events in the coming century are very likely, resulting in potential damage to crops and property, soil erosion, surface and groundwater contamination, and increased risk of human death and injury.

What scientists think is possible...

- Arctic late-summer sea ice may disappear almost entirely by the end of the 21st century (Figure 3).

- Current global model studies project that the Antarctic ice sheet will remain too cold for widespread surface melting and gain mass due to increased snowfall. However, net loss of ice mass could occur if dynamical ice discharge dominates the ice sheet mass balance.

- Model-based projections of global average sea level rise at the end of the 21st century range from 0.18 to 0.59 meters, depending on specific emissions scenarios (Table 2). These projections may actually underestimate future sea level rise because they do not include potential feedbacks or full effects of changes in ice sheet flow.

- Partial loss of ice sheets and/or the thermal expansion of seawater over very long time scales could result in meters of sea level rise, major changes in coastlines and inundation of low-lying areas, with greatest effects in river deltas and low-lying islands.

C. Vegetation and Wildlife

What scientists know...

- Temperature increases have affected Arctic and Antarctic ecosystems and predator species at high levels of the food web.

- Changes in water temperature, salinity, oxygen levels, circulation, and ice cover in marine and freshwater ecosystems have resulted in shifts in ranges and changes in algal, plankton, and fish abundance in high-latitude oceans; increases in algal and zooplankton abundance in high-latitude and high-altitude lakes; and range shifts and earlier fish migrations in rivers.

- High-latitude (cooler) ocean waters are currently acidified enough to start dissolving pteropods; open water marine snails which are one of the primary food sources of young salmon and mackerel (Fabry et al. 2008, Feely et al. 2008). In lower latitude (warmer) waters, by the end of this century Humboldt squid's metabolic rate will be reduced by 31% and activity levels by 45% due to reduced pH, leading to squid retreating at night to shallower waters to feed and replenish oxygen levels (Rosa and Seibel 2008).

- A meta-analysis of climate change effects on range boundaries in Northern Hemisphere species of birds, butterflies, and alpine herbs shows an average shift of 6.1 kilometers per decade northward (or 6.1 meters per decade upward), and a mean shift toward earlier onset of spring events (frog breeding, bird nesting, first flowering, tree budburst, and arrival of migrant butterflies and birds) of 2.3 days per decade (Parmesan and Yohe 2003).

- Poleward range shifts of individual species and expansions of warm-adapted communities have been documented on all continents and in most of the major oceans of the world (Parmesan 2006).

- Satellite observations since 1980 indicate a trend in many regions toward earlier greening of vegetation in the spring linked to longer thermal growing seasons resulting from recent warming.

- Over the past 50 years humans have changed ecosystems more rapidly and extensively than in any previous period of human history, primarily as the result of growing demands for food, fresh water, timber, fiber, and fuel. This has resulted in a substantial and largely irreversible loss of Earth's biodiversity

- Although the relationships have not been quantified, it is known that loss of intact ecosystems results in a reduction in ecosystem services (clean water, carbon sequestration, waste decomposition, crop pollination, etc.).

What scientists think is likely...

- The resilience of many ecosystems is likely to be exceeded this century by an unprecedented combination of climate change, associated disturbance (flooding, drought, wildfire, insects, ocean acidification) and other global change drivers (land use change, pollution, habitat fragmentation, invasive species, resource over-exploitation) (Figure 6).

- Exceedance of ecosystem resilience may be characterized by threshold-type responses such as extinctions, disruption of ecological interactions, and major changes in ecosystem structure and disturbance regimes.

- Net carbon uptake by terrestrial ecosystems is likely to peak before mid-century and then weaken or reverse, amplifying climate changes. By 2100 the terrestrial biosphere is likely to become a carbon source.

- Increases in global average temperature above 1.5 to 2.5°C and concurrent atmospheric CO_2 concentrations are projected to result in major changes in ecosystem structure and function, species' ecological interactions, and species' geographical ranges. Negative consequences are projected for species biodiversity and ecosystem goods and services.

- Model projections for increased atmospheric CO_2 concentration and global temperatures significantly exceed values for at least the past 420,000 years, the period during which more extant marine organisms evolved. Under expected 21st century conditions it is likely that global warming and ocean acidification will compromise carbonate accretion, resulting in less diverse reef communities and failure of some existing carbonate reef structures. Climate changes will likely exacerbate local stresses from declining water quality and overexploitation of key species (Hoegh-Guldberg et al. 2007).

- Ecosystems likely to be significantly impacted by changing climatic conditions include:

i. Terrestrial – tundra, boreal forest, and mountain regions (sensitivity to warming); Mediterranean-type ecosystems and tropical rainforests (decreased rainfall)

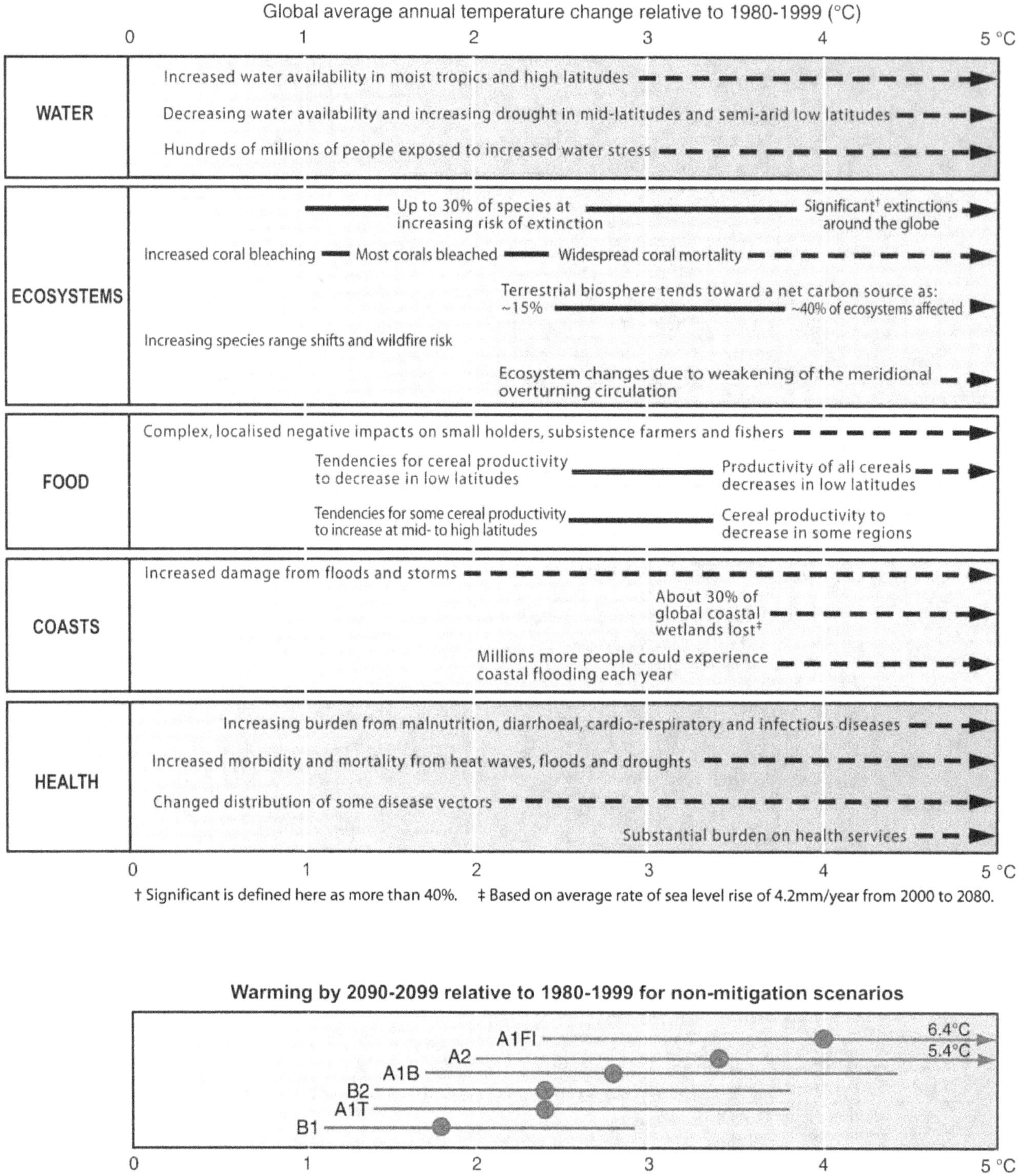

Global average annual temperature change relative to 1980-1999 (°C)

0   1   2   3   4   5 °C

WATER

Increased water availability in moist tropics and high latitudes ➤

Decreasing water availability and increasing drought in mid-latitudes and semi-arid low latitudes ➤

Hundreds of millions of people exposed to increased water stress ➤

ECOSYSTEMS

Up to 30% of species at increasing risk of extinction — Significant[†] extinctions around the globe ➤

Increased coral bleaching — Most corals bleached — Widespread coral mortality ➤

Terrestrial biosphere tends toward a net carbon source as:
~15% ———— ~40% of ecosystems affected ➤

Increasing species range shifts and wildfire risk

Ecosystem changes due to weakening of the meridional overturning circulation ➤

FOOD

Complex, localised negative impacts on small holders, subsistence farmers and fishers ➤

Tendencies for cereal productivity to decrease in low latitudes ———— Productivity of all cereals decreases in low latitudes ➤

Tendencies for some cereal productivity to increase at mid- to high latitudes ———— Cereal productivity to decrease in some regions

COASTS

Increased damage from floods and storms ➤

About 30% of global coastal wetlands lost[‡] ➤

Millions more people could experience coastal flooding each year ➤

HEALTH

Increasing burden from malnutrition, diarrhoeal, cardio-respiratory and infectious diseases ➤

Increased morbidity and mortality from heat waves, floods and droughts ➤

Changed distribution of some disease vectors ➤

Substantial burden on health services ➤

0   1   2   3   4   5 °C

† Significant is defined here as more than 40%.   ‡ Based on average rate of sea level rise of 4.2mm/year from 2000 to 2080.

Warming by 2090-2099 relative to 1980-1999 for non-mitigation scenarios

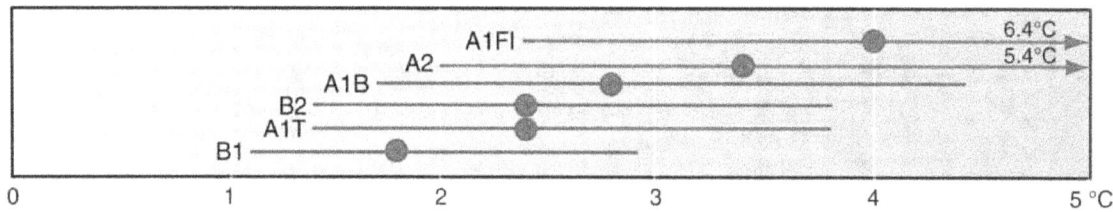

A1FI ———————— 6.4°C
A2 ———————— 5.4°C
A1B
B2
A1T
B1

0   1   2   3   4   5 °C

Figure 6. Examples of impacts associated with projected global average surface warming. Upper panel: Illustrative examples of global impacts projected for climate changes (and sea level and atmospheric CO_2 where relevant) associated with different amounts of increase in global average surface temperature in the 21st century. The black lines link impacts; broken-line arrows indicate impacts continuing with increasing temperature. Entries are placed so that the left-hand side of text indicates the approximate level of warming that is associated with the onset of a given impact. Quantitative entries for water scarcity and flooding represent the additional impacts of climate change relative to the conditions projected across the range of SRES scenarios A1FI, A2, B1 and B2. Adaptation to climate change is not included in these estimations. Confidence levels for all statements are high. Lower panel: Dots and bars indicate the best estimate and likely ranges of warming assessed for the six SRES marker scenarios for 2090-2099 relative to 1980-1999 (IPCC 2007a).

ii. Coastal – mangroves and salt marshes (multiple stresses)

iii. Marine – coral reefs (multiple stresses); sea-ice biomes (sensitivity to warming)

What scientists think is possible...

- Approximately 20% to 30% of plant and animal species assessed to date are at increased risk of extinction with increases in global average temperature in excess of 1.5 to 2.5°C.

- Endemic species may be more vulnerable to climate changes, and therefore at higher risk for extinction, because they may have evolved in locations where paleo-climatic conditions have been stable.

- Although there is great uncertainty about how forests will respond to changing climate and increasing levels of atmospheric CO_2, the factors that are most typically predicted to influence forests are increased fire, increased drought, and greater vulnerability to insects and disease (Brown 2008).

- If atmospheric CO_2 levels reach 450 ppm (projected to occur by 2030–2040 at the current emissions rates), reefs may experience rapid and terminal decline worldwide from multiple climate change-related direct and indirect effects including mass bleaching, ocean acidification, damage to shallow reef communities, reduction of biodiversity, and extinctions. (Veron et al. 2009). At atmospheric CO_2 levels of 560 ppmv, calcification of tropical corals is expected to decline by 30%, and loss of coral structure in areas of high erosion may outpace coral growth. With unabated CO_2 emissions, 70% of the presently known reef locations (including cold-water corals) will be in corrosive waters by the end of this century (Riebesell, et al. 2009).

D. Disturbance

What scientists know...

- Climate change currently contributes to the global burden of disease and premature death through exposure to extreme events and changes in water and air quality, food quality and quantity, ecosystems, agriculture, and economy (Parry et al. 2007).

- The most vulnerable industries, settlements, and societies are generally those in coastal and river flood plains, those whose economies are closely linked with climate-sensitive resources, and those in areas prone to extreme weather events.

- By 2080-2090 millions more people than today are projected to experience flooding due to sea level rise, especially those in the low-lying megadeltas of Asia and Africa and on small islands.

- Climate change affects the function and operation of existing water infrastructure and water management practices, aggravating the impacts of population growth, changing economic activity, land-use change, and urbanization.

What scientists think is likely...

- Up to 20% of the world's population will live in areas where river flood potential could increase by 2080-2090, with major consequences for human health, physical infrastructure, water quality, and resource availability.

- The health status of millions of people is projected to be affected by climate change, through increases in malnutrition; increased deaths, disease, and injury due to extreme weather events; increased burden of diarrheal diseases; increased cardio-respiratory disease due to higher concentrations of ground-level ozone in urban areas; and altered spatial distribution of vector-borne diseases.

- Risk of hunger is projected to increase at lower latitudes, especially in seasonally dry and tropical regions.

What scientists think is possible...

- Although many diseases are projected to increase in scope and incidence as the result of climate changes, lack of appropriate longitudinal data on climate change-related health impacts precludes definitive assessment.

V. References

Allen, C. D., et al. (2010). A global overview of drought and heat-induced tree mortality reveals emerging climate change risks for forests, Forest Ecology and Management, 259(4), 660-684.

Amelung, B., S. Nicholls, and D. Viner (2007). Implications of global climate change for tourism flows and seasonality, Journal of Travel Research, 45(3), 285.

Brown, R. (2008). The implications of climate change for conservation, restoration, and management of National Forest lands. National Forest Restoration Collaborative.

Bourque, C. P. A., R. M. Cox, D. J. Allen, P. A. Arp, and F. R. Meng (2005). Spatial extent of winter thaw events in eastern North America: historical weather records in relation to yellow birch decline, Global Change Biology, 11(9), 1477-1492.

Burakowski, E. A., C. P. Wake, B. Braswell, and D. P. Brown (2008). Trends in wintertime climate in the northeastern United States: 1965–2005, J. Geophys. Res., 113(D20), D20114.

Burns, C. E., K. M. Johnston, and O. J. Schmitz (2003). Global climate change and mammalian species diversity in U.S. national parks, Proceedings of the National Academy of Sciences, 100(20), 11474-11477.

Butler, C. J. (2003). The disproportionate effect of global warming on the arrival dates of short-distance migratory birds in North America, Ibis, 145(3), 484-495.

Campbell, J., et al. (2009). Consequences of climate change for biogeochemical cycling in forests of northeastern North America Canadian Journal of Forest Research, 39 (2), 264-284.

Clark, M. E., K. A. Rose, D. A. Levine, and W. W. Hargrove (2001). Predicting Climate Change Effects on Appalachian Trout: Combining GIS and Individual-Based Modeling, Ecological Applications, 11(1), 161-178.

Currie, D. J. (2001). Projected Effects of Climate Change on Patterns of Vertebrate and Tree Species Richness in the Conterminous United States, Ecosystems, 4(3), 216-225.

Dale, V. H., M. L. Tharp, K. O. Lannom, and D. G. Hodges (2010). Modeling transient response of forests to climate change, Science of the Total Environment, 408(8), 1888-1901.

DeGaetano, A. T., and R. J. Allen (2002). Trends in Twentieth-Century Temperature Extremes across the United States, Journal of Climate, 15(22), 3188-3205.

Deutsch, C. A., J. J. Tewksbury, R. B. Huey, K. S. Sheldon, C. K. Ghalambor, D. C. Haak, and P. R. Martin (2008). Impacts of climate warming on terrestrial ectotherms across latitude, edited, National Academy of Sciences.

Diffenbaugh, N. S., J. S. Pal, R. J. Trapp, and F. Giorgi (2005). Fine-scale processes regulate the response of extreme events to global climate change, Proceedings of the National Academy of Sciences, 102(44), 15774-15778.

Dukes, J. S., et al. (2009). Responses of insect pests, pathogens, and invasive plant species to climate change in the forests of northeastern North America: What can we predict?, Canadian Journal of Forest Research, 39, 231-248.

Fabry, V.J, B.A. Seibel, R.A. Feely, and J.C. Orr. (2008). Impacts of ocean acidification on marine fauna and ecosystem processes. ICES Journal of Marine Science 65: 414-432.

Feely, R.A., C.L. Sabine, J. M. Hernandez-Ayon, D. Lanson and B. Hales. (2008). Evidence for upwelling of corrosive "acidified" water onto the continental shelf. Science 320(5882): 1490-1492.

Field, C. B., L. D. Mortsch, M. Brklacich, D. L. Forbes, P. Kovacs, J. A. Patz, S. W. Running, and M. J. Scott (2007). North America. Climate change 2007: Impacts, adaptation and vulnerability. Contribution of Working Group II to the Fourth Assessment Report of the Intergovernmental Panel on Climate Change, edited by M. L. Parry, O. F. Canziani, J. P. Palutikof, P. J. v. d. Linden and C. E. Hanson, pp. 617-652, IPCC, Cambridge, UK.

Finucane, M. L. (2009). Why Science Alone Won't Solve the Climate Crisis: Managing Climate Risks in the Pacific, 8 pp.

Flebbe, P. A., L. D. Roghair, and J. L. Bruggink (2006). Spatial Modeling to Project Southern Appalachian Trout Distribution in a Warmer Climate, Transactions of the American Fisheries Society, 135(5), 1371-1382.

Frumhoff, P. C., J. J. McCarthy, J. M. Melillo, S. C. Moser, and D. J. Wuebbles (2007). Confronting climate change in the US Northeast: Science, impacts, and solutions, 146 pp, Union of Concerned Scientists (UCS), Cambridge, MA.

Gatewood, A. G., et al. (2009). Climate and Tick Seasonality Are Predictors of Borrelia burgdorferi Genotype Distribution, Appl. Environ. Microbiol., 75(8), 2476-2483.

Griffiths, M. L., and R. S. Bradley (2007). Variations of Twentieth-Century Temperature and Precipitation Extreme Indicators in the Northeast United States, Journal of Climate, 20(21), 5401-5417.

Gu, L., P. J. Hanson, W. M. Post, D. P. Kaiser, B. Yang, R. Nemani, S. G. Pallardy, and T. Meyers (2008). The 2007 Eastern US Spring Freeze: Increased Cold Damage in a Warming World, BioScience, 58(3), 253-262.

Hayhoe, K., C. P. Wake, B. Anderson, J. Bradbury, A. DeGaetano, A. Hertel, X. Z. Liang, E. Maurer, D. Wuebbles, and J. Zhu (2006). Quantifying the Regional Impacts of Global Climate Change: Evaluating AOGCM Simulations of Past and Future Trends in Temperature, Precipitation, and Atmospheric Circulation in the Northeast, Bulletin of the American Meteorological Society.

Hayhoe, K., et al. (2007). Past and future changes in climate and hydrological indicators in the US Northeast, Climate Dynamics, 28, 381-407.

Hayhoe, K., C. Wake, B. Anderson, X.-Z. Liang, E. Maurer, J. Zhu, J. Bradbury, A. DeGaetano, A. Stoner, and D. Wuebbles (2008). Regional climate change projections for the Northeast USA, Mitigation and Adaptation Strategies for Global Change, 13(5), 425-436.

Hester, K. C., E. T. Peltzer, W. J. Kirkwood and P. G. Brewer. (2008). Unanticipated consequences of ocean acidification: A noisier ocean at lower pH. Geophysical Research Letters 35: L19601.

Hoegh-Guldberg, O., P. J. Mumby, A. J. Hooten, R. S. Steneck, P. Greenfield, E. Gomez, C. D. Harvell, P. F. Sale, A. J. Edwards, and K. Caldeira. (2007). Coral reefs under rapid climate change and ocean acidification. Science 318:1737.

Hodgkins, G. A., and R. W. Dudley (2006). Changes in late-winter snowpack depth, water equivalent, and density in Maine, 1926-2004, Hydrological Processes, 20(4), 741-751.

Hopkinson, C. S., A. E. Lugo, M. Alber, A. P. Covich, and S. J. Van Bloem (2008). Forecasting effects of sea-level rise and windstorms on coastal and inland ecosystems, Frontiers in Ecology and the Environment, 6(5), 255-263.

Huntington, T. G., G. A. Hodgkins, and R. W. Dudley (2003). Historical Trend in River Ice Thickness and Coherence in Hydroclimatological Trends in Maine, Climatic Change, 61(1), 217-236.

Huntington, T. G., G. A. Hodgkins, B. D. Keim, and R. W. Dudley (2004). Changes in the Proportion of Precipitation Occurring as Snow in New England (1949–2000), Journal of Climate, 17(13), 2626-2636.

Huntington, T. G., A. D. Richardson, K. J. McGuire, and K. Hayhoe (2009). Climate and hydrological changes in the northeastern United States: recent trends and implications for forested and aquatic ecosystems, Canadian Journal of Forest Research, 39, 199-212.

IPCC (Intergovernmental Panel on Climate Change) (2008). Climate Change and Water, 210 pp, IPCC Secretariat, Geneva.

IPCC (Intergovernmental Panel on Climate Change) (2007a). Climate Change 2007: The Physical Science Basis. Contribution of Working Group I to the Fourth Assessment Report of the Intergovernmental Panel on Climate Change [IPCC, S., D. Qin, M. Manning, Z. Chen, M. Marquis, K.B. Averyt, M. Tignor and H.L. Miller, editors.] Cambridge University Press, Cambridge, United Kingdom and New York, NY, USA, 996 pp. Available at http://ipcc-wg1.ucar.edu/wg1/wg1-report.html (accessed 26 June 2007).

IPCC (Intergovernmental Panel on Climate Change) (2007b). Climate Change 2007 - Impacts, Adaptation and Vulnerability: Working Group II contribution to the Fourth Assessment Report of the Intergovernmental Panel on Climate Change (Climate Change 2007) [Adger, N. et al., editors]. Cambridge University Press, New York. Available at: http://www.ipcc.ch/SPM13apr07.pdf (accessed 3 July 2007).

Iverson, L. R., and A. M. Prasad (2002). Potential redistribution of tree species habitat under five climate change scenarios in the eastern US, Forest Ecology and Management, 155(1-3), 205-222.

Iverson, L. R., M. W. Schwartz, and A. M. Prasad (2004). Potential colonization of newly available tree-species habitat under climate change: An analysis for five eastern US species, Landscape Ecology, 19(7), 787-799.

Iverson, L. R., A. M. Prasad, S. N. Matthews, and M. Peters (2008). Estimating potential habitat for 134 eastern US tree species under six climate scenarios, Forest Ecology and Management, 254(3), 390-406.

Lafon, C., J. Hoss, and H. Grissino-Mayer (2005). The Contemporary Fire Regime of the Central Appalachian Mountains and its Relation to Climate, Physical Geography, 26(2), 126-146.

Lenihan, J. M., D. Bachelet, R. P. Neilson, and R. Drapek (2008). Simulated response of conterminous United States ecosystems to climate change at different levels of fire suppression, CO_2 emission rate, and growth response to CO_2, Global and Planetary Change, 64, 16-25.

McNeil, B. I. and R. J. Matear (2007). Climate change feedbacks on future oceanic acidification. Tellus 59B: 191–198.

Miller-Rushing, A. J., T. L. Lloyd-Evans, R. B. Primack, and P. Satzinger (2008). Bird migration times, climate change, and changing population sizes, Global Change Biology, 14(9), 1959-1972.

Mohan, J. E., R. M. Cox, and L. R. Iverson (2009). Composition and carbon dynamics of forests in northeastern North America in a future, warmer world, Canadian Journal of Forest Research, 39, 213-230.

NABCI (2010). The State of the Birds 2010 Report on Climate Change United States. The State of the Birds. A. F. King. Washington, DC, Department of the Interior, North American Bird Conservation Initiative.

NRC. (2008). Ecological impacts of climate change. The National Academies Press, Washington, D.C.

NSIDC. (2008). National Snow and Ice Data Center.

Orr, J. C., V. J. Fabry, O. Aumont, L. Bopp, S. C. Doney, R. A. Feely, A. Gnanadesikan, N. Gruber, A. Ishida and F. Joos. (2005). Anthropogenic ocean acidification over the twenty-first century and its impact on calcifying organisms. Nature 437(29): 681-686.

Parmesan, C. (2006a). Ecological and Evolutionary Responses to Recent Climate Change, The Annual Review of Ecology, Evolution, and Systematics, 637-669.

Parmesan, C. (2006b). Ecological and Evolutionary Responses to Recent Climate Change, Annual Review of Ecology, Evolution and Systematics, 637-669.

Parmesan, C. and G. Yohe. (2003). A globally coherent fingerprint of climate change impacts across natural systems. Nature 421:37-42. Abstract available at http://www.nature.com/nature/journal/v421/n6918/abs/nature01286.html (accessed 26 June 2007).

Parry, M. L., O. F. Canziani, J. P. Palutikof, and Co-authors. (2007). Technical Summary. Climate Change 2007: Impacts, Adaptation and Vulnerability. Contribution of Working Group II to the Fourth Assessment Report of the Intergovernmental Panel on Climate Change, M.L. Parry, O.F. Canziani, J.P. Palutikof, P.J. van der Linden and C.E. Hanson, Eds., Cambridge University Press, Cambridge, UK, 23-78.

Riebesell, U., A. Kortzinger and A. Oschlies. (2009). Sensitivities of marine carbon fluxes to ocean change. Proceedings of the National Academy of Sciences 106(49): 20602–20609.

Rosa, R. and B.A. Seibel. (2008). Synergistic effects of climate-related variables suggest future physiological impairment in a top oceanic predator. PNAS 105(52): 20776-20780.

Sabine, C. L., R. A. Feely, N. Gruber, R. M. Key, K. Lee, J. L. Bullister, R. Wanninkhof, C. S. Wong, D. W. R. Wallace, B. Tilbrook, F. J. Millero, T.-H. Peng, A. Kozyr, T. Ono and A. F. Rios. (2004). The Oceanic Sink for Anthropogenic CO2. 2004 305: 367-371.

Scott, D., J. Dawson, and B. Jones (2008). Climate change vulnerability of the US Northeast winter recreation– tourism sector, Mitigation and Adaptation Strategies for Global Change, 13(5), 577-596.

Sekercioglu, C. H., S. H. Schneider, J. P. Fay, and S. R. Loarie (2007). Climate change, elevational range shifts, and bird extinctions, Conservation Biology, 1-11.

Smith, J. B., R. Richels, and B. Miller (2001). Chapter 8: Potential consequences of climate variability and change for the Western United States, in Climate Change Impacts on the United States: The Potential Consequences of Climate Variability and Change. National Assessment Foundation Report, National Assessment Synthesis Team, edited, pp. 219-245, US Global Change Research Program.

Speer, J. H., H. D. Grissino-Mayer, K. H. Orvis, and C. H. Greenberg (2009). Climate response of five oak species in the eastern deciduous forest of the southern Appalachian Mountains, USA, Canadian Journal of Forest Research, 39, 507-518.

Tran, J. K., T. Ylioja, R. F. Billings, J. Regniere, and M. P. Ayres (2007). Impact of minimum winter temperatures on the population dynamics of Dendroctonus frontalis, Ecological Applications, 17(3), 882-899.

UNESCO (2007). Climate Change and World Heritage, 51 pp, UNESCO World Heritage Centre, Vilnius, Lithuania.

USDA (2001). Forests: the potential consequences of climate variability and change. A report of the National Forest assessment for the US Global Change Research Program.

USGCRP (2009). Global Climate Change Impacts in the United States. United States Global Change Research Program.

Van Buskirk, J., R. S. Mulvihill, and R. C. Leberman (2010). Declining body sizes in North American birds associated with climate change, Oikos, 119(6), 1047-1055.

Veron, J. E. N., O. Hoegh-Guldberg, T. M. Lenton, J. M. Lough, D. O. Obura, P. Pearce-Kelly, C. R. C. Sheppard, M. Spalding, M. G. Stafford-Smith and A. D. Rogers. (2009). The coral reef crisis: The critical importance of <350 ppm CO2. Marine Pollution Bulletin 58: 1428–1436.

Walther, G. R., E. Post, P. Convey, A. Menzel, C. Parmesan, T. J. C. Beebee, J. M. Fromentin, O. Hoegh-Guldberg, and F. Bairlein (2002). Ecological responses to recent climate change, Nature, 416, 389-395.

Willis, C. G., B. Ruhfel, R. B. Primack, A. J. Miller-Rushing, and C. C. Davis (2008). Phylogenetic patterns of species loss in Thoreau's woods are driven by climate change. Proceedings of the National Academy of Sciences, vol. 105, issue 44, pp. 17029-17033

Willis, C. G., B. R. Ruhfel, R. B. Primack, A. J. Miller-Rushing, J. B. Losos, and C. C. Davis (2010). Favorable Climate Change Response Explains Non-Native Species' Success in Thoreau's Woods, PLoS ONE, 5(1), e8878.

Winnett, S. M. (1998). Potential effects of climate change on U.S. forests: a review, Climate Research, 11, 39-49.

Wolfe, D., L. Ziska, C. Petzoldt, A. Seaman, L. Chase, and K. Hayhoe (2008). Projected change in climate thresholds in the Northeastern U.S.: implications for crops, pests, livestock, and farmers, Mitigation and Adaptation Strategies for Global Change, 13(5), 555-575.

Wuebbles, D. J., and K. Hayhoe (2004). Climate change projections for the United States Midwest, Mitigation and Adaptation Strategies for Global Change, 9(4), 335-363.

Ziska, L., P. Epstein, and C. Rogers (2008). Climate change, aerobiology, and public health in the Northeast United States, Mitigation and Adaptation Strategies for Global Change, 13(5), 607-613.

Zuckerberg, B., A. M. Woods, and W. F. Porter (2009). Poleward shifts in breeding bird distributions in New York State, Global Change Biology, 15(8), 1866-1883.

NPS 909/111736, November 2011